Map from Goode's World Atlas
© 1992 by Rand McNally, R.L. 92-S-85

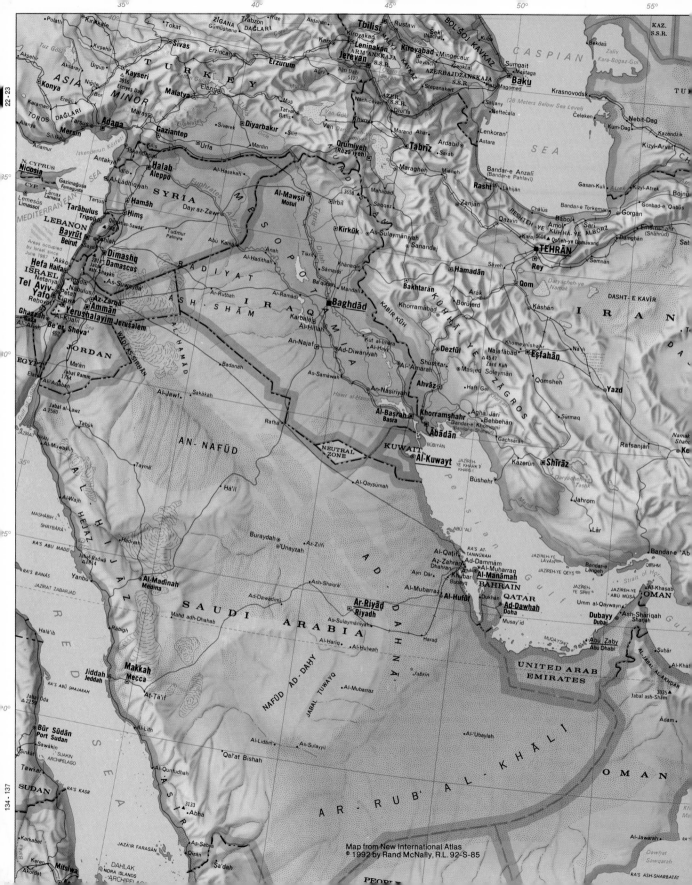

Enchantment of the World

BAHRAIN

By Mary Virginia Fox

Consultant for Bahrain: John Duke Anthony, Ph.D., President, National Council on U.S.-Arab Relations, Washington, D.C.

Consultant for Reading: Robert L. Hillerich, Ph.D., Visiting Professor, University of South Florida; Consultant, Pinellas County Schools, Florida

CHILDRENS PRESS®

CHICAGO

Young boys are dressed in the long outer garment called a thobe.

Project Editor: Mary Reidy
Design: Margrit Fiddle

Library of Congress Cataloging-in-Publication Data

Fox, Mary Virginia.
    Bahrain / by Mary Virginia Fox.
        p.   cm. — (Enchantment of the world)
    Includes index.
    Summary: Describes the history, geography, culture,
government, and industry of the island country in the
Persian Gulf.
    ISBN 0-516-02608-9
    1. Bahrain—Juvenile literature. [1. Bahrain.]
I. Title. II. Series
DS247.B2F69   1992   92-8892
953.65—dc20   CIP
                                                      AC

Picture Acknowledgments
AP/Wide World Photos: 1, 11, 19, 26, 41, 42 (bottom), 44,
46, 53, 66 (top), 67 (inset), 68, 101
The Bettmann Archive: 34
Courtesy of Gulf Air: 5, 6 (bottom), 9, 59 (right), 65 (top),
66 (bottom left & right), 69, 78 (2 photos), 79, 87 (2
photos), 89 (bottom right), 91 (2 photos), 96, 106 (top
inset)
Historical Pictures Service/Chicago: 29, 36 (inset), 38
Reuters/Bettmann: 42 (top)
Root Resources: © **John S. Major,** 36, 49, 55 (2 photos), 64
(top), 89 (left); © **Robert Biggs,** 80, 89 (top right)
Tom Stack & Associates: © **Byron Augustin,** Cover, 33, 59
(left), 62, 64 (bottom left & right), 95 (right), 97, 105, 106
(bottom inset), 108
SuperStock International, Inc.: © **Wim Berssenbrugge,** 12,
51, 68 (inset), 70 (right), 71, 74, 76, 95 (left), 98 (bottom);
© **J. Baker,** 17; © **David Forbert,** 52, 104; © **Kurt Scholz,** 63
(top), 106 (center); © **G. Ricatto,** 65 (bottom), 67, 107
TSW-CLICK/Chicago: © **Tom Sheppard,** 4, 50; © **Jane
Lewis,** 15; © **Nabeel Turner,** 32; © **David McDowall,** 92
UPI/Bettmann: 45
Valan: © **Christine Osborne,** 8, 23 (2 photos), 60, 63
(bottom), 73, 83, 98 (top), 103; © **A. B. Joyce,** 70 (left);
© **Kennon Cooke,** 72 (left); © **Paul L. Janosi,** 72 (right);
© **K. Ghani,** 100
Len W. Meents: Maps on 8, 13, 46
**Courtesy Flag Research Center, Winchester,
Massachusetts 01890:** Flag on page 6 (inset) and back
cover
Cover: Al Fatah Mosque, Manama, Bahrain

Basket weavers practice an age-old craft.

TABLE OF CONTENTS

Above: Bank buildings in downtown Manama
Below: Bahrain has one of the world's largest oil refineries.

Chapter 1

A DESERT SURROUNDED
BY WATER

ANCIENT HISTORY

Considering its size, *Bahrain* ("two seas") has had a tremendous influence on the world. Its own history has been traced back more than five thousand years to Sumerian times. Because of its strategic position in the Persian Gulf, also called the Arabian Gulf, it has always been a major port of the sea trade.

The Phoenicians used it as a safe harbor to replenish water supplies. The islands were visited by ships of Alexander the Great in the third century B.C.; later the Portuguese, who dominated the sea for profit during the Middle Ages, anchored here. Pirates used Bahrain as a base to attack ships that sailed the sea-lanes to and from the riches of India and beyond. Now huge oil tankers are serviced in Bahrain's modern dry-dock facilities.

In the past, Bahrain's riches were measured by its water supply and pearls from the offshore oyster beds. Today modest oil production, an oil refinery, an aluminum smelter, and numerous banks are the source of most of the country's revenue.

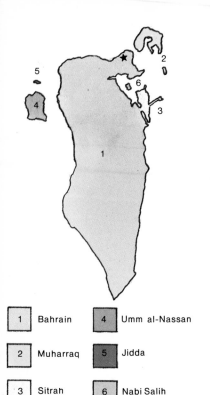

1	Bahrain	4	Umm al-Nassan
2	Muharraq	5	Jidda
3	Sitrah	6	Nabi Salih

★ Manama

Manama is located on the northeast shore of the big island.

A CHAIN OF ISLANDS

The Bahrain archipelago lies between Saudi Arabia and the Qatar Peninsula. The group includes six principal islands— Bahrain, Muharraq, Sitrah, Umm al-Nassan, Jidda, and Nabi Salih—and twenty-seven minor islands, including the Muhammadiyah and Hawar groups. The total area is 262 square miles (678 square kilometers), only a speck on the globe, but it is a speck that has dominated the history of the region.

Bahrain, by far the largest of the islands, gave the entire archipelago its name. Manama, the capital of the country, is located on the northeast shore of the big island. A causeway, 1.5 miles (2 kilometers) long, connects Bahrain to the second-most-important island, Muharraq. Sitrah is joined to Bahrain by a bridge.

A monument to the ancient civilization of Dilmun, which is mentioned in Babylonian and Sumerian records

The most impressive transportation link with the Arabian Peninsula, a fourteen-mile (twenty-three-kilometer) causeway to Saudi Arabia, the ancestral home of Bahrain's ruling family, was completed in 1986. The Saudis financed the billion-dollar span.

At one time the Arabian Peninsula's entire northern coastal region was known as Bahrain. Bahrain itself was called Dilmun. Sumerian poems from the *Epic of Gilgamesh* describe Dilmun as the island of immortals, to which heroes were transported to live in eternal bliss.

CLIMATE

From a Westerner's point of view, Bahrain seems like a strange Garden of Eden. It is a desert land surrounded by water. Its climate varies from sweltering high humidity in the summer to damp chill in the winter months, when the thermometer drops to around fifty degrees Fahrenheit (ten degrees Celsius).

It is during these months that the scant rainfall, averaging 3 inches (7.6 centimeters) a year, occurs. As long as Bahrain's Civil Aeronautics Weather Bureau has been keeping records, there has never been a rainfall during June, July, August, or September.

Prevailing winds, known as *gaws*, are from the southwest. Bahrain can be swept by blinding sandstorms. It is not unusual for a ship sailing several miles out in the gulf to be blasted by a wall of sand. When the gaws blow, there is nothing to block them as they sweep across the desert because the highest elevation in the islands is Jabal Dukhan, rising 445 feet (136 meters) above the landscape.

From the mainland of Saudi Arabia, Bahrain appears to be no more than a smudge on the horizon, a sea-bound oasis bordered with a coastline of crumbling limestone and sand. It may seem surprising that such a land would produce an advanced civilization, but geologists reason that the local climate has changed over the past five thousand years. They can tell by the slant of the old sand dunes, stabilized with sparse vegetation over the years, that the winds once came from the northeast, which would have provided a more temperate climate.

THE GIFT OF FRESH WATER

Even in today's different environment, there are areas irrigated by artesian wells at the north end of Bahrain island that nourish the country's numerous date-palm groves.

The most remarkable of Bahrain's water wells are the submarine springs that exist just offshore. Fresh water bubbles up

Water from an underground well is pumped into an
old bathtub, which serves as a trough for this burro.

beneath the sea in such abundance that the islanders can wade out
into the saltwater sea and fill their jars with fresh drinking water.
The wells are marked with iron posts, pounded into the seabed,
that extend above the surface of the water.

Bahrainis have always regarded water as a gift from the gods
and long ago had a simple explanation for how it happened.
Falling stars must have knocked holes in the ground, they said,
and Allah cupped them up for the use of his faithful followers.
Some said there had to be a hole in the Shatt-al-Arab, the lower
reaches of the Euphrates River, which empties into the head of the
gulf, thus spilling its fresh water into an underground river that
surfaces in this holy spot.

The finding of water has always been important in early
legends. Sumerians, who lived at the head of the gulf, believed
that the earth and sea rested upon another sea, the *Abuz*. Unlike
the ordinary sea, which is salt, the Abuz was fresh water. The god
of the Abuz, also known as *Abyss*, was a god whom it was
important to please. The word abyss is the only Sumerian word

A *desalination plant at Sitrah*

that has entered the English language, although it has been changed to mean any bottomless depth.

Today geologists have solved the riddle. They know that the source of the water is in the Tuwaiq Mountains, some 250 miles (402 kilometers) west of Qatif, Saudi Arabia. It then seeps through porous levels of rock in the direction of lucky Bahrain.

Whatever the explanation, the water is there and is being used lavishly with the expansion of a modern urban civilization. Bahrain's government and the population are conscious of the need to conserve their precious water resources. Since 1985, Bahrain has placed increased emphasis on the development of desalination units to extract pure water from the sea. Although it is costly to build and maintain such modern technological devices, all agree that the expense of having them is a necessity, not a luxury.

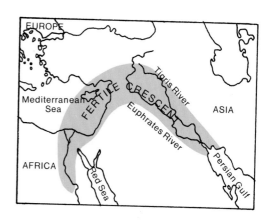

Chapter 2

IN THE BEGINNING

DILMUN

Scholars may disagree about the location of the beginning of the human race, but there is no disagreement that the cradle of civilization lies in an area in the Middle East called the *Fertile Crescent.* That area includes Mesopotamia (modern Iraq), Syria, Palestine, Anatolia (eastern Turkey), and Persia (Iran). Bahrain lies close to this realm.

Much of Europe was covered by a sheet of ice, but to the south, in Africa and Arabia, the climate was favorable for the transition from a life of nomadic wandering to a civilization where groups of people could come together and develop permanent settlements.

One of the earliest great civilizations was developed by the Sumerians at the head of the Arabian Gulf, in the watershed of the

Tigris and Euphrates rivers. They built great palaces, temples, and libraries. Their records were kept on clay tablets written in *cuneiform* ("wedge-shaped") script. Some of the tablets told stories of the history of the land and its heroes.

THE FLOOD

Both the Assyrians and Sumerians wrote their own accounts of the "Great Deluge," which are much the same as the biblical story of Noah and the Flood in the Christian and Jewish religions.

It was said that Enki, the god of the water under the earth, warned a man named Uti-nipishtim that the world was to be destroyed because of the evil deeds of those around him. He was told to build an ark and take his family and his livestock on board.

For six days and six nights the tempest raged. On the seventh day the ark grounded on a mountaintop in upper Kurdistan. A dove and a swallow were sent out, but returned. Later a raven was released. When it did not come back, Uti-nipishtim knew that the water had receded. He left the ark and made sacrifices to the gods in thanks for his safety.

Enki, the god of water, spoke to Enlil, the greatest god of all, and made Enlil promise that never again would he punish all of mankind for the sins of some. To make up for the cruelty of his previous act, Enlil met with Uti-nipishtim and his wife and touched them both on the forehead. He promised they would never die. "Now he and his wife be like gods; and they shall dwell in the distance at the mouth of the rivers."

The Sumerian version called the chosen man Ziusudra. "The Ziusudra, the king, the preserver of the name of vegetation and of the seed of mankind, will dwell in the land of the crossing, the land of Dilmun, the place where the sun rises."

Archaeologists have dug up and studied the area that was called Dilmun.

The story goes on to say that "Dilmun is holy. Dilmun is pure. The lion kills not. The wolf snatches not the lamb." It was a land where there was no sickness, no old age.

"Let your wells of bitter water become wells of sweet water. Let your furrowed fields and acres yield you their grain. Let your city become the dock yard house of the land." Archaeologists are convinced that this magical kingdom where men came to seek immortality is what we now know as Bahrain.

THE SEARCH FOR IMMORTALITY

Among the clay tablets archaeologists found what many believe is the earliest epic story that we know of, the *Epic of Gilgamesh*. Gilgamesh was a hero of ancient Sumeria. The epic tells about his deeds and about his search for the land where he could become immortal. Gilgamesh went to visit Uti-nipishtim, who had been given everlasting life, to find out how he could be blessed the same way. Uti-nipishtim promised that if Gilgamesh followed instructions he would find the flower of immortality and unheard of riches. It was said that the flower grew on the seabed.

Gilgamesh was to attach stones to his feet so that he would sink to the ocean floor, where he could pluck the magical flower. He was promised that if he ate a pearl inside the flower, his youth would be renewed.

However, there is no happy ending to the story of Gilgamesh. He followed instructions and plucked the flower from the seabed, but he decided to take it home to share with the elders of his native city, Erech. When he slept, a snake came up from the water hole. As in Genesis in the Bible story of Adam and Eve, the snake cheated mankind out of eternal life. The snake ate the pearl, and thereby achieved immortality itself. Even today whenever the snake feels itself growing old, it sheds its skin and emerges young and vigorous again. The moral of the story is very clear: How can man, who cannot conquer sleep, hope to conquer death?

THE MAGIC LAND

Why do we think that today's Bahrain is the location of the legendary land of Dilmun? Bahrain lies southeast of the mouth of the rivers, far from the mountain where the ark is supposed to have landed.

The Arabian Gulf was known by three names: the Lower Sea, the Bitter Sea, and the Sea of the Rising Sun, which could have referred to the body of water, not the direction. Of course, the main reason we think of the island as the magic land is because of its water supply, unequaled any place else along the gulf shores.

A merchant weighing some pearls.

Bahrain is surrounded by the largest pearl oyster beds anywhere around. It also contains the largest cemetery of the ancient world—facts that Gilgamesh and his countrymen well knew.

A MAMMOTH CEMETERY

In a very small area, there are more than 170,000 burial mounds, varying in size from mere bumps on the desert landscape to mounds as high as forty feet (twelve meters), which cover elaborate burial chambers. From the air it is an even more startling sight—clusters of burial mounds that emboss the gravel landscape like pages from a book written in braille.

With such a wealth of material, it would seem easy to piece together the story of this strange land. But grave robbers have been pillaging the mounds for at least the past three thousand years.

What archaeologists have been able to determine is that the people seemed to be normally healthy and died of natural causes. Their average height was about 5 feet 8 inches (1.73 meters). They must have been moderately wealthy to afford such elaborate burials. Many are entombed in chambers of heavy stone.

The few pieces of jewelry that were found were of fine workmanship and may have come from distant areas. Lapis lazuli would only have been found in the Indus Valley region of India, and the bronze daggers must certainly have been imported.

One of the most exciting discoveries unearthed is a small temple with a stone altar and a seat that was probably reserved for a god. Pottery, lapis lazuli beads, alabaster vases, and a copper figure of a bird were found here. One would guess that worshipers would stand here before the god bearing offerings. There also was a small copper statue of a naked man, standing in just such an attitude of supplication. It was not unusual to leave a figure behind to remind the god of the prayers that were being said.

What baffles the experts is why such a small island would have so many human remains. Did it mean that those from the mainland sought burial in this consecrated place, or was this the home of a large population? As records from the Sumerians show that Dilmun was a busy trading port, both answers may be true.

HELP FOR ARCHAEOLOGISTS

Today, electrical currents are archaeologists' eyes, helping them to map the area. Remote pictures from satellites in outer space have given scientists an overall image of the Bahrain graveyards. Airplanes scouting for potential oil-bearing regions have been used to photograph a more detailed picture of the area,

A French archaeological team examines the remains of a four-thousand-year-old temple. In the background is the reconstructed wall of a Portuguese fort.

numbering the exact location of each mound. Close-up views by ground-sensing instruments carried on the shoulders of scientists have shown where burial chambers are located within the mounds.

These instruments, called EM-31s, or Non-contacting Terrain Conductivity Meters, consist of two arms that extend about 5 feet (1.5 meters) from the instrument box. The transmitting arm sends an electrical current into the ground and produces a magnetic field, which tells the operator whether the ground beneath his feet is dense or made up of loosely packed soil and whether there are stone blocks or cavities in the earth.

Computers analyze the data and produce three-dimensional contour maps. In some cases, they can even determine if the graves have been disturbed and robbed. These new technologies have saved hundreds of hours of backbreaking, often useless, digging. They have meant that archaeologists have not destroyed the very remains they have been seeking, as was often the case in earlier years. Digging into huge piles of rubble, no matter how careful the intentions of the diggers, has often broken up the evidence they were seeking.

ANCIENT CREDIT CARDS

Some of the most interesting artifacts recovered have been small seals. They are carved out of either shell or stone. Most are no more than three or four inches (eight or ten centimeters) long, round or oblong, usually with a hole in one corner so that they could be laced with a thong and carried around one's neck or waist. Each merchant or trader had his own individual identification. When shipments of goods were sent from one port to another, the seal was imprinted on wet clay that was attached to the shipment. These seals were zealously guarded and handed down from one family member to another.

Translations of clay tablets have recorded that a man whose seal held the form of a ram sold ingots of bronze to a merchant whose seal had the sign of a fish. There was no source of this metal on the barren shores of Bahrain, but as a well-known exchange port, goods from all over must have passed through it.

Sumerians are known to have been the first civilization to use stamped silver bars for money. They also employed letters of credit, lending money to neighboring people at interest rates of 20 to 30 percent. Gold and copper were both mined in Arabia. The busy trading port of Dilmun must certainly have been involved in the transfer of goods and services. At least one silver bar was recently unearthed that had been missed by grave robbers long ago.

Chapter 3

SACRED OBJECTS

PEARLS

Water was indeed a blessing for Bahrain, but vanity and the wish for some rare prize brought fame and riches to those who could furnish a king's or queen's treasure. No one knows when the first pearl from Arabian waters was pried from its shell, but ancient history records a number of famous people who flaunted their wealth by collecting these gems from the sea.

Ishtar, a Babylonian goddess-princess, was said to have a necklace of pearls so long that even when she stood, they brushed the ground. And it has been written that the Queen of Sheba owned black pearls from the waters of Bahrain. Cleopatra is supposed to have eaten crushed pearls, probably in the hope of making the legend of Gilgamesh come true.

Huge piles of oyster shells have been found in the remains of coastal villages in Bahrain, dating back as far as 3000 B.C. In those days divers brought their oysters ashore and let them bake in the sun before opening them for the prize. Today's divers are more apt to split the shells as soon as they are brought up, throwing the discards overboard.

A century ago, as many as five thousand small boats with slanted triangles of canvas sailed from Bahrain for a three-to-four-month season of "pearling." Before leaving port, the sailors treated the upper hulls of their boats with evil-smelling shark oil, which keeps the deck wood from cracking in the intense heat from the sun. They painted the underwater part of the hulls with lime and sheep fat to discourage barnacles.

Each boat carried from six to fifteen men. Many died each year from the bites of sharks and poisonous sea snakes and the stings of poisonous rays and jellyfish. Scurvy and skin troubles also took their toll, but there was always the hope of riches. In 1929 one gulf pearl sold for as much as $100,000. This was a rare find.

Equipment for pearl diving was simple: bone or tortoiseshell nose clips, leather thimbles to protect fingers from sharp coral, and a wad of beeswax in each ear. Fifty dives a day were usual.

Divers worked in water anywhere from 5 to 20 fathoms (9 to 37 meters) deep; a fathom measures 6 feet (1.8 meters). The best oysters seemed to be found at the deepest depths. It was a dangerous trade. Divers carried a basket with them to haul up the catch, and each diver had a lifeline attached to his wrist. When he was ready to come up with his harvest, or when danger threatened, he jerked on the lifeline. The best divers were able to remain underwater for up to two minutes.

When the pearls were brought to shore, they were sorted in low sheds on the beach, carefully watched by boat owners so that no special prize slipped past the sorting sieve. A small brass plate with different-sized holes was used for sorting the gems. Black pearls were considered bad luck by Arabs, but they brought top prices from jewelry buyers around the world.

Oysters must be pried open to take out the pearls (left). The pearls are sorted and graded (above) before they are sold.

COMPETITION

Although profits from the sale of the catch were shared by the crew, a diver's share rarely covered the food or expenses advanced to him by the *nakhuda,* or captain. Inevitably the diver was committed to work for the next season and the next.

During the 1930s pearl prices fell when Japanese cultured pearls flooded the market. Today the pearling trade is just a memory, but one that is kept alive by retired divers and captains who meet at their favorite coffee shop to dance and sing traditional chanteys. To the sound of a lute, the rhythm of drums, and the hand clapping of watchers, men dressed in long gowns and head cloths whirl and leap in a surprising show of vigorous athletics.

The songs tell of the old pearling days when the waters were crystal clear and pearls the size of hens' eggs were set in crowns around the world. The singers seem to have forgotten sleeping on hard decks, eating meals of only fish and dates, and having to overcome the constant fear of underwater dangers.

But Bahraini pearls are still a collector's item. Some wealthy Arabs carry short strings of pearls to count off verses when reciting prayers, as Catholics use their rosaries. In this case, however, the strings link eleven, twenty-two, or thirty-three pearls or beads, evenly divided denominations of what Muslims hold to be at least ninety-nine attributes of God (for example, the Merciful, the Compassionate). For some, the pearls are often fingered as a means, not always conscious, of relieving tension.

SUPERNATURAL POWERS

Pearls have always had a mystical quality. Some have been given supernatural powers, according to their owners. A well-known soothsayer in the marketplace of Manama swears he can find lost articles by merely clutching his magic pearl in his hand.

It also has been said that if a young woman rubs her eyes with a pearl, she can merely gaze at a man and make him her slave. Of course, it has to be a pearl of the right size, and she will probably have to pay the owner of that pearl a considerable price for such strong magic. But if one can believe that pearls are formed by mermaids' tears that fall into the oyster while the shell is open, then almost anything can be believed.

PRE-ISLAMIC DESERT LIFE

Pearls are not the only prized objects in a gulf Arab's life. The Bedouins who roamed the desert believed they were surrounded by a host of spirits, or *jinn*. Before the coming of Islam, these spirits were cornerstones of religious life. The Bedouins worshiped in a series of sacred places, frequently marked only by a circle of stones. There was no need or wish to build a cathedral. The spirits worshiped were part of nature.

The desert Arabs were self-sufficient. They lived by a code of bravery, hospitality, and the inviolate honor of the family and the tribe. Their religion was primitive and an integral part of their lives.

Tribal laws were strict, and punishment to right a wrong, to correct an injustice, was severe—something that is true to this day. Murder or rape were punished by beheading the guilty one if he were a man. On the rare occasion that a woman was found guilty of infidelity, she would be stoned to death. The family of the victim had the right to be the executioner. It was a strict code. Life for many was interspersed with cycles of vengeance. An attack on any clan member was treated as though it were an attack on all of the clan—the same concept, in the name of collective security, that many centuries later modern statesmen have tried to integrate into the United Nations system.

An individual convicted of theft might have his hand severed. The hand would then be hung on a pole outside the dwelling of the thief's family as a way of shaming his relatives and as a warning to the public in general that under no circumstances would theft be condoned.

HOSPITALITY

Such punishment may seem excessive to some, but not to those who can identify with the harsh environment the Bedouins endured. People then generally had so few belongings that any

Sheep breeders provide the Bahrainis with lamb, their meat of choice.

kind of theft could not be tolerated. To steal someone's sheep might leave that person's family to die.

At the other end of the scale, Arabian hospitality has never been equaled. A stranded traveler would be taken in and treated as one of the family, traditionally for at least three days, long enough for him to eat well, rest, and be restored so he could continue his journey. Even during periods of low provisions, when sharing meant hunger for the host family, generosity was extended.

In today's Arab world, it is considered an insult for one's guest to decline an invitation to share food or even a cool drink or a cup of coffee.

THE BEDOUIN

The term Bedouin suggests to many a picture of a wandering family of herdsmen. Frequently it was not a way of life of their choosing. Arabs from the mainland found a more settled life-style in Bahrain. Although the famous water wells made agriculture possible, there was not enough irrigated land for everyone.

Great care was taken to distribute the water to as many people as possible. Under the intense desert sun, water in irrigation ditches evaporated before it could be directed to crops, so an intricate series of tunnels was dug to channel the water from the wells. The tunnels were built on a slight downward slope, with gravity facilitating the water's flow from one location to the next. Some of these ancient waterworks, called *ganats*, were built around 3000 B.C. and many still are being used today.

Most of the immigrants to the islands came to join the fishing or pearling fleets or to work as paid employees of the merchants. Some became boat builders.

OTHER INFLUENCES

From the Stone Age until the era of Islam, Bahrain was influenced by the Babylonian, Assyrian, and Greek civilizations, but it remained a separate entity. Both in ancient history and officially until as recently as 1970, Persia, now Iran, claimed Bahrain. Persia was nearby, on the other side of the gulf. It was a country that once was so strong that its empire reached from the Mediterranean Sea to the Indian Ocean. But after Persia's fall from world power, the Greeks and Romans took the principal role in fostering an elite culture. Greek geographers gave Bahrain still another name on their maps, Tylos.

But Bahrain was so small in comparison to neighboring lands that it was left to govern itself. Bahrain's closest ties were to the Arabian mainland, where caravans crossed the forbidding desert that shielded them from the rest of the world.

The coming of the Prophet Muhammad, who spread the religion of Islam, was the most important event in all of Middle Eastern history. Bahrain was part of that religious movement.

Chapter 4

PRAISE ALLAH

ISLAM

Because of its vastness, the geography of the area, and the resulting nomadic life-style of the Bedouin, the Arabian Peninsula as a whole—a landmass greater than all of Western Europe combined—never had a unifying culture or government until the Islamic religion forged its migratory and settled groups into a single political entity.

It was true that there were prosperous trading centers dominated by powerful merchants, but the ruling families of such centers frequently collapsed when succeeding generations failed to supply a strong leader. Their subjects were taxed in return for protection from neighboring warring tribes, but if the tribute the rulers sought to collect was too harsh, the loyalty of their subjects changed rapidly.

Islam was born in the seventh century A.D. in Mecca, in what is now Saudi Arabia. The religion emerged during a period of conflict that is remarkably similar to some of the problems of the

A traditional Arabian caravan

present—new wealth versus traditional values. The city of Mecca was both a center of pilgrimage focused on the gods of that era and a stopping place for fabled camel caravans. Many of the caravans carried goods from India and central Africa to Mecca. From there, goods were often transported to ports on the Mediterranean. Like any other thriving commercial center, Mecca attracted thieves and speculators along with a variety of merchants and others who were trying to earn an honest living.

MUHAMMAD IS BORN

Sometime during A.D. 570 or 571, Muhammad bin Abdullah bin Abd al-Muttalib bin Hashim was born. He was orphaned at age six and lived with his grandfather, a devout man who claimed to be a direct descendant of Ishmael, son of Abraham and Hagar.

In his middle years Muhammad began to retreat into the hills surrounding Mecca for long periods of meditation. During one of these periods, he claimed that the Angel Gabriel appeared in a vision and revealed a new religion from Allah (the Arabic word for God). Although Muhammad could not read or write, his followers recorded the words of the revelation, which were collected in the holy book, the *Koran.*

ONE GOD

Islam means "submission to the will of God." There is only one Supreme Being, Allah to the Muslims, God to Christians, and Yahweh to the Jews. In Islam, there is neither a priesthood nor a papacy, for no man or organization should stand between the believer and God. Jesus and Moses are regarded as prophets, just as Muhammad is.

Certain commandments about charity and love of one's fellowman carry much the same meaning as those written in the commandments given to Moses. Muhammad's description of paradise as the reward of a true believer is similar to the Christian picture of heaven.

Muslims are enjoined to pray five times a day, bowing their heads to the ground and facing Mecca, which Muhammad had consecrated as a holy city. Muslims annually observe a whole month of fasting, when from sunup to sundown, no food or water may be consumed. This is known as the month of *Ramadan.* Muslims are also required to contribute annually at least 2.5 percent of their net wealth to the poor and to complete a pilgrimage *(hajj)* to Mecca at least once in their lifetime. Muslims regard Friday as their holy day of the week.

ABRAHAM'S DESCENDANTS

Many stories of the Old Testament are also part of Muslim beliefs. Ishmael was born to Hagar and Abraham. Muslims believe that a promised land was to be given to Ishmael and his family. He is considered the father of the Arab nation.

But thirteen years after Ishmael was born, Sarah, Abraham's elderly wife, bore a child named Isaac. According to the Bible, God promised that Isaac would become the father of nations, and that Ishmael would beget twelve princes and establish a great nation.

The land of Canaan, where Judaism and Christianity originated, was held by the twelve tribes of Israel. This area later became known as Palestine. From about A.D. 600 until the mid-1900s, the majority of people in Palestine were Arabs who also considered Palestine a sacred place. The creation of the state of Israel in 1948 and its expansion at the expense of Arab independence, sovereignty, and territorial integrity in 1948-49, 1956, 1967, and 1982 were bitter blows to Arabs.

RELIGIOUS LAW

Islam swept across the Arabian Peninsula and within a century reached southern France and deep into the Indus Valley. Over the years Islamic practices, like those of Christianity and Judaism, have varied over time and from place to place. Saudi Arabia, Bahrain's neighbor, is the most conservative Islamic country. Saudi Arabia, foremost among the world's forty-six Islamic countries—more than a quarter of the members of the United Nations—is guardian of Islam's two holiest sites, Mecca and Medina. Mecca lies in Saudi Arabia's Western Province, forty-

Muslim worshipers in Mecca

eight miles (seventy-seven kilometers) inland from the Red Sea.
Medina is in the same western region, but lies to the north and
farther inland. Medina, the city where the economic, social, and
political dimensions of Islam were first administered by a
government, contains the prophet Muhammad's tomb.

From Mauretania and Morocco in the west to Persia and
Pakistan in the east, and from Baghdad in the north to Berbera in
Somalia in the south, all the Middle Eastern countries embraced
Islam. Islam is much more than a religion, it is an entire way of
life. The Koran not only spells out the religious obligations of the
faithful but also is the primary source for laws.

Islamic law is built on three sources. At the core is the Koran,
the word of God as revealed to Muhammad.

The *Sunna*, which is a collection of lore related to the prophet's

Islam's holy book, the Koran

life and behavior as remembered and recorded by his followers, is the second-most important source of reference for Islamic law and guidance. The *Hadith* are the pronouncements of the prophet as recorded or remembered by his companions. Within a few generations, they were collected, compiled, and catalogued. The Hadith are co-equal with the Sunna as a guide and validator for Islamic law. The Sunna, the Hadith, and the Koran have been incorporated into a body of law called *Sharia*, an Arabic word that means both "street" and "the way." The spirit and in many cases the literal sense of the Sharia is at the heart of both the constitutional and the legal systems of the Muslim world with regard to numerous issues in the realm of social, commercial, domestic, criminal, and political affairs.

Within the body of Islamic thought, there are all kinds of laws

Pious Muslims pray five times a day, no matter where they may be.

that govern personal behavior: the appropriate ways to wash oneself and to display affection, the emphasis on modesty in dress and ornamentation, and certain things that are forbidden; for example, Muslims are not supposed to eat pork or drink alcohol. When the Koran was revealed, the meat from pigs was often the source of disease; and alcohol, then as now, alters one's senses.

Although Islamic life may seem to be strictly regulated by Western standards, a Muslim believes that rules make it easier to reach the perfect life that awaits one in heaven. Human beings and society are by nature imperfect and limited in their ability to always do what is correct and pleasing in the eyes of the Almighty. Therefore, most Muslims believe that a system that contains a measure of discipline, certainty, and predictability and at the same time is humane and just and offers a great deal of freedom within recognized boundaries is a system that is bound to be strong, healthy, and beneficial to people and society as a whole.

From the first call to prayer at dawn to the last after sunset, a pious Muslim's day is punctuated with prayer. Muslim prayer is not a petition for the favors of God; rather, it is a ritual that reminds mere mortals of the power of Allah.

THE HIJRAH CALENDAR

The Islamic calendar, *Hijrah*, dates from A.D. 632, the date when thirty-five members of the original community of Muslims emigrated from Mecca to Medina where they established the first Islamic government. The calendar is governed by the phases of the moon. Three hundred fifty-four days are divided into twelve lunar months. In every Christian century, there are 100 years; during the same period, the Islamic calendar repeats itself 103 times.

Because each year ends approximately twelve days earlier than the previous year, the seasons do not fall in the same months from one year to the next. Ramadan is observed in the ninth month of the Hijrah calendar, the month when the first Koranic verses were revealed to Muhammad.

Ramadan is a rigorous exercise in denial and self-discipline. During daylight hours, a Muslim abstains from all food, drink, and sex. When the month of fasting comes in the heat of the summer, it is an even greater challenge, but a pious Muslim is proud to show his spiritual strength. For virtually every Muslim, Ramadan is a time of spiritual and moral renewal. One counts and appreciates one's many blessings and deepens the compassion felt for those less fortunate.

*Under the leadership of Alfonso d'Albuquerque (inset),
the Portuguese built a fort (above). The ruins have been uncovered
and give evidence it was once an impressive stronghold.*

Chapter 5

THE GOVERNMENT

THE PORTUGUESE ERA

Six years after Columbus discovered America, Vasco da Gama sailed around the southern tip of Africa and discovered the route to India. Phoenicians are said to have made the dangerous passage many years earlier, but da Gama, having enlisted the services of the famed Arab navigator, Ahmad bin Majid, of Oman, was the first European to map the route.

During the following years the Portuguese, under Admiral Alfonso d'Albuquerque, established themselves along the coasts from the Cape of Good Hope to India itself. They built trading posts and controlled harbors where their ships could be resupplied.

In 1521 they sailed into the waters of Bahrain and declared it to be a possession of Portugal. The Bahrainis were no match for the fighting forces the ships brought with them.

The Portuguese built an impressive fort on the highest point of land in the center of the north coast of Bahrain. They chose a spot where Arabs had previously constructed a fortification. Archaeologists digging at the base of one of the square corners of

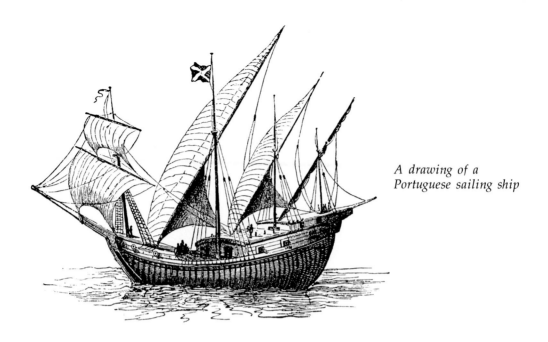

*A drawing of a
Portuguese sailing ship*

the fort towers, which was of European origin, came across the foundation of an earlier round turret, typical of Arab design. The Portuguese obviously used many of the earlier building blocks for their own use.

The Portuguese also dug a moat around the outer wall. It was a well-fortified stronghold.

Trading at this location must have been extensive. Broken pieces of fine Ming porcelain from China are still being found in the ruins.

The conquerors were interested only in control of the sea-lanes, not the lands beyond. By 1602, the Bahrainis, with the help of other Arabs, were able to force the Portuguese to withdraw from their islands, although the Portuguese influence in maritime affairs throughout the gulf still continued to be felt.

PIRATES

The fort on the island of Bahrain remained empty and slowly began to deteriorate, but it was still a great lookout point.

Eventually, it was taken over by bands of pirates who kept track of the sea-lanes in search for heavily laden ships.

To defend themselves, captains of the larger sailing ships armed their vessels with cannons and recruited companies of archers to stand guard when they were in gulf waters. Still the pirates seemed to be winning the battles.

They sailed in small boats called *dhows*, forerunners of many of the sailing craft in the gulf today. They were rigged with triangular sails held up by a long yardarm on a short mast. They handled easily and with a good captain, they could outmaneuver the larger sailing ships.

THE AL-KHALIFA DYNASTY

In 1782 the head of a force directed by leaders of the al-Khalifa Arab family seized the islands with support from neighboring rulers. From then until the present day, the al-Khalifa have remained Bahrain's ruling family. They are cousins of the al-Sabah ruling family of Kuwait and are more distantly related to the ruling family of Saudi Arabia.

PROTECTED BY BRITAIN

As the eighteenth century ended, Great Britain had succeeded other European nations as defender of the sea-lanes on which much of the Western world depended for its survival and prosperity. Britain had been fairly successful in ridding the Mediterranean of the Barbary pirates, but it was impossible to keep patrols on guard all over the world. When and where it could be made to work, diplomacy could be just as efficient and far more cost-effective.

With this objective in mind, Great Britain signed an agreement with the ruler of Bahrain in 1820. Bahrain guaranteed that it would punish those who attacked British shipping. In return, Britain agreed to uphold the sovereignty of Bahrain. Across the waters of the gulf, the shah of Persia, with a fleet at his disposal, had been eyeing other gulf ports covetously. Bahrain was a prize that might easily have been captured had it not been under the protective wing of England.

The Treaty of 1820, as later amended, also specified that the ruler of Bahrain could not dispose of any of his territory except by agreement with Great Britain. He also could not enter into relationships with any foreign government other than Great Britain without British consent.

The Treaty of 1820 was the first of several binding agreements with Britain that were revised in 1861, 1892, and still later in 1951. However Bahrain was never a colony, protectorate, mandate, or trusteeship, of the British. Rather its status in international law was that of a British protected-state.

THE MONARCHY

The al-Khalifa family has ruled Bahrain since the late eighteenth century. During this time the administrative system was developed. Rulership used to be passed on by consultation with the family council and the prominent merchants and religious leaders of the country. At the end of the nineteenth century, however, Shaikh Isa bin Ali al-Khalifa changed this system to avoid family conflicts, from which he himself had suffered when he came to power. Accordingly the elders of

Removing British military equipment and other property from Bahrain in 1971

Bahrain issued a document calling for automatic succession of the eldest son of the ruler.

INDEPENDENCE

In January 1968 Great Britain announced its intentions to withdraw military forces from the area by 1971. In March 1968 Bahrain joined the nearby territories of Qatar and the seven Trucial States (now the United Arab Emirates), which were also under British protection. For a while it was thought that these smaller shaikhdoms might form a federation of their own.

Because of their diverse interests, however, Bahrain and Qatar elected not to join the federation. Bahrain proclaimed its independence as a separate state on August 15, 1971.

A constitution, approved in 1972, included provisions for a

Shaikh Isa bin Salman al-Khalifa, the emir (above), opened a summit conference in 1982. The crown prince, Shaikh Hamad (left), during a 1983 visit to Washington, D.C.

Parliament (National Assembly), the first in the country's history. Elections took place in 1973. The National Assembly consisted of thirty members elected by male citizens for four-year terms, plus as many as sixteen Cabinet ministers.

In August 1975, however, the prime minister submitted his resignation, complaining that his power was being obstructed by the Assembly. The *emir*, or ruler, reinstated the prime minister and abolished the Assembly. In doing so, he reported to the Bahraini people on the danger to national security from several instances of alleged subversive activity among Assembly members. Supposedly, some Assembly members were making overtures to the Iranian government to make Bahrain a territory of that country. The emir has promised new elections, but these have not yet occurred. With the onset of the Iranian revolution in the late 1970s, the eight-year Iran-Iraq War that followed, and the Persian Gulf War, the emir frequently pointed out that the threats to Bahrain's security were not potential but real. As an example, he stated that during World War II Great Britain, the mother of Parliaments, had reasoned that the holding of national elections was an indulgence entailing risks that the government could not afford.

At present, the emir of Bahrain is Shaikh Isa bin Salman al-Khalifa, who is addressed as "Your Highness" or "Shaikh Isa." His brother, Shaikh Khalifa, is the prime minister, and the heir apparent (crown prince) and commander-in-chief of the Bahraini defense force is Shaikh Hamad, Shaikh Isa's eldest son. (The correct pronunciation of shaikh is as if the word were spelled shake.) Commoners fill half the cabinet posts and members of the ruling family fill the rest.

Bahrain's six towns and cities (Manama, Muharraq, Rifa, Gharbi, Sitrah, and Judd Hafs) are administered by municipal

During an audience in the main meeting room of Shaikh Isa's palace, members of government, petitioners, and other guests wait in line around the hall.

councils, the members of which are appointed by the emir. The courts administer the legal code and review the laws to ensure their fairness.

In keeping with the openness, informality, and simplicity of ancient Arab customs, the emir receives petitioners at a regular open house. Anyone in the country has the right to meet with the ruler for any reason. The merits of the system are not only its directness and the leveling effect it has on the relations between rulers and ruled but also the fact that if a request is granted, action can be taken without any bureaucratic red tape. The ruler's aides are present to ensure that requests are routed to the appropriate government agency. Under this system the ruler tries to ensure that the request will receive immediate attention by the appropriate officials and that the petitioner will receive a satisfactory response in seventy hours or less.

Shaikh Isa and President George Bush review United States troops during the emir's visit to Washington, D.C., in 1991.

BAHRAIN AFFAIRS

Bahrain is a member of the United Nations and has lent expertise in several areas to promote improved health and education in the gulf region.

In April 1986, George Bush, then vice-president of the United States, visited Bahrain to reaffirm the United States' readiness to preserve gulf security in the event of an escalation of the Iran-Iraq war.

In January 1987, the United States announced that it was selling twelve F-16 jet fighters to Bahrain, the first gulf country to receive these aircraft. Work immediately began on the construction of an air base in the south of the island to accommodate the planes. Bahrain has allowed United States naval vessels and personnel to use its ports and related facilities. During Operations Desert

Workers cut a rubber "skirt" to form part of a boom to hold back oil spilled during the Persian Gulf War.

Shield and Desert Storm, following Iraq's invasion of Kuwait in August 1990, Bahrain played a major role in the Allied coalition that liberated Kuwait by allowing extensive use of its facilities.

A NEW TOWN

One of the most interesting development projects in Bahrain in recent years has been the construction of a new town, Madinat Hamad, in the middle of the island. One of the objectives was to provide an attractive environment away from the north of the island in Manama and the islands of Sitrah and Muharraq where 80 percent of the population lives.

The land for the new town was donated by the emir, and covers approximately 3,212 acres (1,300 hectares) in an area that was desert before the project began. The town now houses between seventy thousand and eighty thousand Bahrainis. Twelve thousand homes were built by local construction companies under contract to the ministry of housing. This has alleviated the crowding of the nation's capital and provided low to medium-priced housing for those in need.

From north to south, Madinat Hamad is 5 miles (8 kilometers) long and about 1.5 miles (2.5 kilometers) wide. The site is on a plateau, gently sloping to the west, giving some of the inhabitants a panoramic view of the sea. In most parts the soil has been classified as being of potentially little agricultural use.

The town is bordered by natural features such as *wadis*, or dried-up watercourses, that have been retained to carry rainwater. A town center is the focus for shopping and entertainment. Each of the town's four districts has its own range of small shops, mosques, and schools.

When completed, the town will have a five-hundred-bed hospital, three health centers, four secondary schools, six to eight intermediate schools, twenty-two primary schools, three community centers, a library, police and fire stations, five large and about fifty smaller mosques, and numerous playgrounds and playing fields for children and students.

Madinat Hamad is linked to other centers on the island by a new road that provides access to the causeway and joins the new town, as well as Awali and Sitrah, to Manama.

An attractively landscaped boulevard will link all the district centers. Great care has been taken to preserve the ancient grave mounds nearby. A museum and research center will be established to provide for the continuing study of the artifacts found within the mounds.

The qanats, the covered artificial irrigation channels and wells, almost as ancient as the grave sites, also are being restored and retained as features of the town.

Chapter 6

WEALTH COMES TO BAHRAIN

OIL

An enterprising New Zealander, Major Frank Holmes, went to Bahrain in the early 1920s to assist in developing water resources for the country. In studying the geology of the region, he became obsessed with the idea that oil lay in the folds of shale below the surface.

The preliminary surveys of Bahrain were not very encouraging, but Holmes persisted. In 1922, he crossed over to the Arabian mainland and negotiated with Saudi King Abdul Aziz Al Saud for a concession to permit exploratory drilling. The area where drilling was to take place covered more than 30,000 square miles (77,700 square kilometers). The concession was granted in 1923. Two years later Holmes succeeded in obtaining an oil concession in Bahrain.

These agreements were in the name of British investors, who expected quick profits. Although Holmes was not an oil man, he hoped to interest companies with available drilling equipment. He was unsuccessful, however, and his concession on the mainland expired.

Bahrain's first oil well no longer produces, but it is kept as a historical monument.

In the meantime, the Standard Oil Company of California (Socal, or what today also is known as Chevron), one of the largest United States oil producers, had been exploring in eighteen countries, but had found no substantial oil reserves. The Gulf Oil Company of the United States had taken up the option in Bahrain, but with its hands full from fulfilling a commitment to drill in Iraq, it turned its legal rights over to Socal. In turn, Socal established a subsidiary company, the Bahrain Petroleum Company (Bapco) to continue exploration. Bapco, with its United States office in Dallas, Texas, has remained the primary oil company in Bahrain ever since.

THE FIRST WELL

Bahrain's first oil well was drilled in 1931. After less than seven months of drilling, to a depth of 2,008 feet (612 meters), the

A plaque marking oil well number 1

company struck "black gold" and began production at the initial rate of 9,600 barrels a day. The day that oil spewed from the drilling rig in Bahrain was a milestone—not only for the small island country but for the Middle East as a whole. Today a special marker notes that the well at Jabal Dukhan was the first on the Arab side of the gulf. (Iran discovered oil on May 15, 1908.)

Over the years, the technology used in oil production has improved. The number of wells drilled in Bahrain is 310, with 290 producing petroleum and 20 producing gas. The oil field's reserves, never large, have steadily declined, however; for most of the 1980s and into the 1990s production seldom exceeded 45,000 barrels a day—less than 1 percent of Saudi Arabia's average daily production over the same period.

MARKETING THE OIL

When Bapco began operations, it built huge collection tanks, called tank farms, and a pumping station from which to load

An oil refinery in the desert

crude oil directly onto tankers. The first cargo was sold in
December 1934, at roughly midpoint in the decade-long
international economic Depression. In 1935 Bapco built an oil
refinery with the capacity to refine ten thousand barrels a day.
Although the amount was small by today's standards, it was the
first refinery to be constructed on the Arab side of the gulf.

Engineering technology came from several countries, but Great
Britain and the United States were the first to arrive with
blueprints. Bahraini workers were trained in all aspects of the
production. Because many of the workers had formerly been
engaged as fishermen or pearl divers, the economic and social
transformations that came in the wake of the oil industry's early
years in Bahrain were changes that, even today, have not yet run
their course in terms of their impact on Bahraini culture.

Soon after Bahrain began producing oil, Bapco sold half of its
shares to the Texas Company (Texaco) to benefit from Texaco's

A tug guides an oil tanker into port as a fisherman watches.

marketing outlets in Asia, Africa, and Australia. Together Texaco
and Socal set up a new marketing company called California
Texas Oil Company (Caltex), which is still in operation.

PRODUCTION

Oil has proved its worth for more than sixty years, paying more
than 70 percent of the Bahraini government's expenses, despite
the fact that Bahrain's production, as noted, is but a droplet by
Saudi Arabian standards.

Bahrain's overall production developed gradually. From 1948 to

Shaikh Salman, about ten years before his death in 1961

1956 it remained stable at thirty thousand barrels a day, after which it rose to forty-five thousand barrels, where it remained until 1963. Production peaked at seventy-six thousand barrels a day in 1970, before it fell to about forty-seven thousand barrels in the mid-1980s and forty-two thousand barrels in the early 1990s. Single wells in Saudi Arabia and Kuwait produce as much as one-fourth of all of Bahrain's wells combined.

Even so, for such a small country, oil income in any amount was a blessing. During the reign of Shaikh Salman bin Hamad al-Khalifa, from 1942 to 1961, the added income provided for social services and public works that would not have been possible otherwise.

Shaikh Salman died in November 1961 and was succeeded by his eldest son, Shaikh Isa. Now into his fourth decade as head of state, Shaikh Isa has continued to use a large portion of the income generated from petroleum for the good of the country.

Bahrain's oil reserves are expected to be exhausted by about the year 2010. Widespread knowledge of the nearness of that date explains the sense of urgency in Bahrain's search for other ways to produce income.

THE FUTURE OF OIL

In the meantime, Bahrain continues to pump oil. After selling 60 percent of the country's greatly expanded refinery to Bapco in 1980, Caltex now owns only 40 percent of the operation. The refinery exports to the Far East products that range from jet fuel to asphalt. A jetty that extends 3 miles (4.8 kilometers) into the gulf is used for filling deep-draft tankers at the rate of three a day.

Bahrain also received one-half of the net income from the Abu Safah offshore oil field, which was claimed by both Saudi Arabia and Bahrain. An agreement was reached in 1986, under which the output from the field was to be shared equally between them. By 1983 this field accounted for more than 50 percent of Bahrain's revenues from petroleum. However, because of cutbacks to regulate production and limit the supply of oil on the world market, the Abu Safah field was closed down early in 1987. Saudi Arabia agreed to provide seventy-five thousand barrels per day of crude petroleum in compensation, which went directly to the Bahrain refinery.

GAS

The Bahrain National Gas Company operates a gas liquefaction plant that uses oil-associated natural gas piped directly from Bahrain's oil fields. Natural gas is the principal fuel for Bahrain's

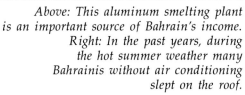

Above: This aluminum smelting plant
is an important source of Bahrain's income.
Right: In the past years, during
the hot summer weather many
Bahrainis without air conditioning
slept on the roof.

aluminum industry. Accordingly, exploration and drilling operations to increase production have expanded. Seventeen new wells were drilled in 1986 and thirteen more the following year. Production has risen gradually to about 450 million cubic feet (12.7 million cubic meters) a day.

The gas is extracted from two geological layers, the Khuff layer and the Arabian layer, which underlie most of the gulf region. Gas is also the primary energy used to run the island's power stations and fuel its seawater desalination plants.

The principal consumer of natural gas is the Aluminum Bahrain Company, using about 150 million cubic feet (4.2 million cubic meters) daily. This is followed by the Bahrain State Electricity Department, which is absorbing increasing quantities of gas, especially during the summer months when the need for air conditioning is greatest.

According to census figures, Bahrain's population increased 245 percent between 1959 and 1981. This rapid rise, combined with an increase of more than 50 percent in water consumption between 1979 and 1983, has necessitated considerable expansion of power and desalination facilities.

By the early 1980s natural gas fueled four of Bahrain's major power stations in four towns, and there are plans for a fifth station to be completed in 1992. The desalination plant at Sitrah is expected to increase capacity to 20 million gallons (76 million liters) a day. It is estimated that at the present rate of consumption, the country's gas reserves will be exhausted by the year 2018.

Like all of its gulf neighbors, Bahrain benefited from the region's economic boom from the mid-1970s to the early 1980s. During that time the government developed many projects to improve the standard of living, with expansion of health and educational services and provisions of better housing among the top priorities. But because of the subsequent worldwide fall in oil prices and depressed energy markets throughout the remainder of the 1980s and into the 1990s, Bahrain has had to tighten its budget and work even harder to diversify its economy.

DIVERSIFICATION

Because Bahrain was already a well-established commercial center, its petroleum industry developed more rapidly than that of other gulf countries. For some years now, Bahrain has refined and shipped oil for others and provided banks to serve their financial needs.

Even before oil was discovered, Bahrain, with a public school system dating from the beginning of the twentieth century, had the highest literacy rate in the Arab world. Dating from an even earlier period, Bahrain assimilated British bureaucracy practices when that nation established military and trading relations with Bahrain. Not surprisingly, English quickly became and has even since remained a second language in the country. Britain had established excellent lines of communication, via telephone and radio, with the outside world. These were all advantages Bahrain had over its neighbors.

BANKING

One of the most important changes in the country came in the mid-1970s. Until 1975, banking in Bahrain was confined to financial institutions serving traders and residents of the island. Banks elsewhere in the gulf region were ill-equipped to cope with the huge exchange of cash and investment certificates generated by the oil-exporting nations.

Beirut, Lebanon, had been a chief banking center, but civil war in Lebanon, which began in 1975 and is only now subsiding, made investment there a risk.

In 1975 the Bahraini government announced the introduction of Offshore Banking Unit (OBU) licenses, which meant that foreign banks could operate without having to meet local ownership requirements. Offshore banking essentially provides a free port for high finance, eliminating burdensome taxes charged elsewhere. The controlling government body is the Bahrain Monetary Agency, which acts as a central clearinghouse and regulates exchange rates.

For nearly a decade, the OBUs gave a substantial boost to Bahrain's economy. Bahrain quickly found itself processing the highest volume of transactions of any financial center in the Middle East. More than 150 international financial houses established offices in Bahrain in the aftermath of Beirut's fall from prominence, from nearby Kuwait and Jordan and from Zurich, Switzerland; New York; London, England; and Hong Kong. Their combined portfolios have at times exceeded 23 billion dollars.

As oil prices climbed after the 1973 embargo, several Middle Eastern oil-producing countries began to accumulate enormous money surpluses. Their governments began looking for a major banking center where clients could deal freely in rials, dirharns, and dinars (money used in the Arab gulf countries) as well as in dollars, British pounds sterling, and other internationally prominent currencies.

Bahrain was a natural to take over, being favorably located in the heart of the Arab business world, especially the countries that make up the Gulf Cooperation Council (GCC): Kuwait, Saudi Arabia, Qatar, Oman, the United Arab Emirates, and itself.

With purchasing power in such strength, it is not surprising that investors have been attracted to the region. The potential for future markets in Iraq and Iran, once stability returns to these countries and Bahrain's and its neighbors' relations with them improve, is a further lure. In the early 1990s, following the reversal of Iraq's aggression against Kuwait, the relations of Bahrain and the other GCC countries with Iran were improving slowly but steadily. The situation in Iraq, however, was by contrast far less settled.

Bahrain is halfway between the financial centers of Europe and the Far East, in the right time zone to cover both money markets during the period from 7:00 A.M. to 7:00 P.M. The OBUs lend, take deposits, and trade currencies for foreign corporations and nations in a tax-free, no-reserve setting. For instance, if a foreign exchange dealer at the Citibank OBU sees a favorable exchange rate from

Two of the banks in Manama are the National Bank of Bahrain (left) and Arab Banking Corporation (above).

Singapore, instantaneous direct-dial telephone, telex, and fax communications are channeled by Bahrain's own earth-satellite station to make the transaction.

The British Bank of the Middle East is the oldest international bank in Manama. Its respect for the heritage of the country is symbolized by the architecture of the building that houses the company. Its massive bronze doors are decorated with copies of seals of the ancient civilization, the same seals that enabled the handling of foreign transactions in ancient times.

The Gulf International Bank is owned collectively by seven gulf countries (Bahrain, Iraq, Kuwait, Oman, Qatar, Saudi Arabia, and the United Arab Emirates) and is a wholesale bank. Its customers are other banks and governments. In the early 1990s, Bahrain established a stock exchange.

Already the world's top banks in Bahrain are linked to major capital cities. International firms of lawyers, accountants, and consultants provide further services to a modern business center.

King Fahd Causeway connects Bahrain with the mainland at Saudi Arabia.

Chapter 7

A FAST PACE

THE CAUSEWAY

For centuries Bahrain's destiny has frequently been influenced by developments on the mainland of the Arabian Peninsula. Its ruling family hails from the same central Arabian plateau as the Sa'ud ruling family of Saudi Arabia. Both countries share a desert heritage and are governed by Islamic laws. Only a small stretch of water separates them.

Since 1986 the two have been physically linked via a causeway. Built at a cost of over a billion dollars, the fourteen-mile (twenty-three-kilometer) roadway includes two bridges, one with a forty-foot (twelve-meter) clearance for larger boats. The entire cost of the project was financed by Saudi Arabia.

The link, officially known as the King Fahd Causeway, has opened markets that were previously impractical for Bahraini merchants and traders. Today many Western firms are making Bahrain their base camp for business expansion in the region. Tourism, trade, and commerce have increased substantially.

When land within the capital's limits became scarce, engineers simply diked in large areas, pumped out the water, filled the areas

A night view of al Fatah Mosque

with plenty of available sand and gravel, and offered them for building properties. More than seven square miles (eighteen square kilometers) have been reclaimed over the past ten years.

These coastal zones were reserved mainly for heavy and light manufacturing and industry that need access to port facilities. Bahrain's first major industrial area was established close to the port of Mina Salman in 1960. Within two years it was full, and expansion continued. Today there are also "specialist zones" for light industries like handicrafts and woodwork in support of traditional artisan activity.

THE FACE OF THE CITY

Approaching Bahrain along the new King Fahd Causeway from Saudi Arabia gives one the sensation of skimming over water. What lies ahead is a flat, sun-parched land with only a fringe of greenery that has been irrigated. To the visitor, this seems unimpressive from a distance.

Manama is built on the northeast shoreline of the big island.

A busy, congested section of Manama (above) and a modern department store (below)

Above: During the intense heat at midday, not many people are in the market. Below: Outdoor sculptures include a monument to pearl diving (left) and a tea pot (right)

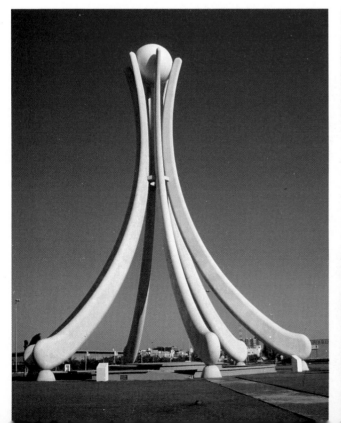

A colorful amusement park (above) and the Bahrain Monetary Agency (below)

Above: A contrast in the lifestyles of Bahrain—a man leads his donkey cart past a parked Rolls-Royce
Below: Useful items for sale in the market (left) and buildings in Manama's diplomatic area (right)

The minaret of this mosque towers over the other buildings.
Inset: A businessman steps out of his Mercedes-Benz.

The skyline is a mixture of past and present. Tall minarets that spike the sky beside the city's mosques stand side by side with the massive cubes of mortar and glass that house the impressive office buildings and banks of Bahrain's new wealth. Huge derricks from the shipyards share the horizon with the stacks and pipes of the great refinery near Sitrah to the south.

In Manama, some fifty thousand cars, many of them Mercedes-Benzes and Rolls-Royces, tangle with traffic, which has been growing at a rate of about 10 percent per year. There are 140 miles (225 kilometers) of roads surfaced in asphalt, which is relatively low priced in Bahrain. These roads are more than adequate for the small size of the country, and an enormous increase since the days of travel by donkey.

Officials and business executives consult the board at the Bahrain Stock Exchange. A satellite station (right) enables Bahrain to have an excellent communication system.

COMMUNICATION

Bahrain has one of the most modern communication systems in the world. It has two satellite stations in outer space that provide links between the Middle East and the rest of the world. The first was installed in 1968, the second in 1980. There is direct-dial telephone service to more than fifty countries, as well as telegraph, telex, fax, and data-base exchange services to nearly two dozen global centers.

What makes these new developments so mind-boggling is to know that most Bahraini men over forty years of age have memories of making their own shoes. The Industrial Revolution, which in Europe developed over several generations, is being compressed into a matter of a relatively few years in Bahrain. While much is made of the difference between parents and

Gulf Air serves India, Saudi Arabia, other Middle Eastern countries, as well as Asian and European cities.

children in Western countries, imagine the far greater differences between Bahrain's older generations and its modern-day youth in their respective experiences regarding education, upbringing, and standards of living.

Bahrain's thirty-five thousand television sets pick up six color channels from its own station and those of neighboring countries. Bahrain's first daily newspaper in Arabic, *Akhbar Al-Khalij*, began publication in 1976 and the first English daily, *The Gulf Daily News*, in 1978.

TRANSPORTATION

In 1991 a new terminal was added to the international airport, located on the island of Muharraq. Twenty-two major airlines make regularly scheduled stops in Bahrain. Bahrain was the first

Buildings at the Bahrain airport (left) and the highway (right) that connects Awali, in the center of Bahrain, with Zallaq on the coast

airport in the world to receive scheduled Concorde aircraft flights, linking London to the Middle East in two hours. Bahrain lies on the main round-the-world air route. London and the Far East are only about four hours away aboard the Concorde. More than three million air passengers are processed through Bahrain every year.

Bahrain has the reputation of being the air capital of the Arabian Gulf. One reason is the state-of-the-art equipment used by Bahrain Airport Services (BAS). BAS is a private firm that employs more than eighteen hundred employees to handle traffic, cargo, engineering problems, and food catering.

Recently the cargo terminal underwent an expansion of 280,000 square feet (26,000 square meters) to house custom activities to ensure that merchandise is speedily dispatched. The terminal has streamlined its handling procedures with the latest mechanized cargo-handling equipment, facilities for special cargo that must be

The seaport at Mina Salman

chilled or frozen, and space for livestock and hazardous goods. Its food service for connecting flights provides more than ten thousand meals daily.

Mina Salman, the country's most important port, was built by the Bahraini government to the east of the capital of Manama. It was opened by His Highness the Emir Shaikh Isa bin Salman al-Khalifa on May 31, 1962.

Although the port is one of the most modern and efficient ports in the Middle East, it has been undergoing major extension and redevelopment ever since it was opened. Mina Salman now provides sixteen deep-water berths where ships can unload cargo directly into the port's storehouses.

Northeast of Sitrah are the docks for vessels transporting oil products and aluminum. Another port, just north of Manama, was built in the 1930s, and is still busily in use. All these ports are run entirely by Bahrainis in the manner of their ancestors since the days of Dilmun.

The date palm (left) provides fruit and also produces material used to weave baskets, mats, wall hangings, and make chicken coops and other household items.
Above: The red hibiscus blossom

AGRICULTURE

One consequence of Bahrain's increasing urbanization is that less and less of its land is used for agriculture. To the south and east of the capital city, however, are the gardens of wealthy citizens. The vivid green of jasmine and the red of hibiscus and ripening pepper trees brighten the gray-green of the date palms. Here it does look like a Garden of Eden.

The development of agriculture in general, however, is limited by the scarcity of water and the salinity of the soil. Apart from the narrow strip of fertile land in the north, the rest of the island is mainly bare of vegetation. Continuous development seeks to boost the country's food production and reduce the dependency on food imports through the extension of high-tech farming techniques.

Men making a wire trap used in fishing

FISHING

The government also gives priority to Bahrain's fishing industry. Under an assistance program, materials needed by fishermen can be purchased on a 50-percent subsidy, and a mobile workshop exists to provide on-the-spot service for the fishing fleet.

LABOR

Westerners, whether advisers, consultants, or full-time employees, have been classified as highly paid servants but treated cordially, because they contribute valuable expertise to a country anxious to reap the benefits of the most modern technology available.

A pipeline from Saudi Arabia

Most manual laborers in Bahrain are from lesser developed countries. The great majority are recruited for nonpermanent assignments and, as temporary workers, may not purchase real estate or apply for citizenship. Some Muslims, who come from far away to make the pilgrimage to Mecca, stay to earn their transportation home. Some laborers are Africans, and still others are Koreans, Filipinos, Thais, and other Asians who are "pushed" by the lack of economic opportunities at home and "pulled" by the lure of lucrative jobs in places like Bahrain, where the Bahrain dinar is easily convertible into very valuable hard currency that is in much demand in the emigrants' home countries.

INDUSTRY

Bahrain's ministry of development and industry foresees a bright future for the country, and many foreign investors and other business leaders agree with its assessment.

Bahrain went from oil production into oil refining, then into manufacturing products such as ammonia, methane, alcohol, and

74

aluminum. Now, in preparing for the second step in its industrialization, Bahrain intends to produce new technologies needed in the Middle East.

Bahrain, with one of the oldest oil refineries in the world, has started to manufacture the instrumentation for petrochemical and oil-refining plants. The process involves the implementation of state-of-the-art technology. Computers control the temperature, flow, and movement of liquids. Bahraini engineers and technicians have learned by experience, and are ready to share that experience with others for a profit.

Bahrain, in a joint venture with Kuwait and Saudi Arabia, has entered a new era with the manufacture of plastics and petrochemicals, two fields that hold much promise for the future.

ALUMINUM

When Bahrain needed expert advice in setting up its enormous aluminum plant, it turned to the United States and West Germany. The Bahrain government owns about four-fifths of the vast facility of Aluminum Bahrain (Alba); a United States firm, Kaiser Aluminum, holds 17 percent; and a West German firm, 5 percent. Recently Bahrain offered Saudi Arabia a share of the 230 million dollar smelter to help finance a profitable expansion.

Already the plant houses a 0.5 miles (0.8 kilometer) production line. The profitability of the operation was increased by expansion. By adding only a hundred people to the work force— less than 5 percent—Alba has been able to increase production by 30 percent. By saving a hundred dollars a ton, Alba has become the competition to beat in world markets.

Other related factories are the Aluminum Extrusion Company

Part of Bahrain's dry dock, one of the largest in the world

and the Gulf Aluminum Rolling Mill. They take the raw product from the smelter and turn it into forms for the manufacture of specific items. There is also the Arab Iron and Steel Company, which takes iron ore and converts it into pellet form.

SHIPBUILDING

Another industrial venture is Bahrain's 340 million dollar Arab Shipbuilding and Repair Yard (ASRY). It is used by all gulf nation oil producers that require transportation for their crude product. Tankers are the main method of transporting oil to market.

Bahrain turned to the Organization of Arab Petroleum Countries (OAPEC) for help in OAPEC's first joint venture. Although built on Bahraini land, Bahrain's fellow OAPEC members—Algeria, Egypt, Iraq, Kuwait, Libya, Qatar, Saudi Arabia, and the United Arab Emirates—helped finance the venture.

In 1974 a Dutch dredging firm began creating a hundred-acre (forty-hectare) island and connecting it to Muharraq, a small island four miles (six kilometers) to the north and east of Manama. Then an army of two thousand South Korean workers erected the docks and workshops.

The main dry dock is one of the largest in the world—longer than four football fields placed end to end. A mammoth tanker needing repair is floated into the dock. Three pumps suck the water out from beneath the ship. These pumps have enough suction power to empty an Olympic-size pool in one minute.

Huge cranes handle pieces of equipment that range from entire engine assemblies to slabs of steel decking.

By mid-1976 a team from Portugal's Lishave, the world's largest ship-repair yard, arrived to manage the site. Sixteen months later ASRY opened its locks to its first supertanker—three months ahead of schedule.

While much expertise was imported from other countries, it was the vision and original planning of Bahraini executives who got the project going and coordinated every step of the way. Bahrain is a logical location for such a facility. It is situated near the middle of the gulf, the world's busiest thoroughfare for oil-tanker traffic.

The fifteen-hundred-man staff covers all phases of marine engineering, from steel plate and pipe work to electronics and major engine repairs. When the Iran-Iraq war of the 1980s resulted in damage to tankers in the area, the shipyards worked overtime. A dozen different languages can be heard at any one time, from Filipino tugboat captains to Portuguese, German, and English technicians conversing with their Bahraini counterparts in strained Arabic.

Small ships are constructed with as much care as are large ones. Wooden dhows are made the same as they were in antiquity, long before the advent of Islam.

Few dhows continue to carry sails; motors have been in use for decades.

THE SMALL SHIPS

Not only huge ships receive care in these waters. The boat works near Manama's central market are busy turning out wooden dhows in the same style that has been in use since antiquity. The family trees of some of these boat builders can be traced back through the centuries. The same skills and the same knowledge have been passed from one generation to the next. Workers hew frames from mangrove roots to brace the teak planking added later.

Some dhows are still equipped with sails, but the great majority of captains rely on motors, which are simpler, faster, and cheaper in the long run. A large dhow needs a crew of six or more to sail; only two are needed with motor power.

In keeping with age-old customs regarding modesty, many Bahraini women wear veils in public.

Chapter 8

THE PEOPLE OF BAHRAIN

NEW AND OLD

Bahrain is a study in contrasts. It has always been among the more cosmopolitan of the Arab countries because merchants, traders, and sailors have brought it into contact with people from distant places. Yet among its citizens, from the ruling family to those in the working class, are many devout Muslims, whose life-style is, at least in part, determined by the rules of the Koran.

The more conservative religious leaders of Bahrain's closest neighbor, Saudi Arabia, have periodically criticized Bahrain for not being as strict in its enforcement of religious laws. Saudis have been regarded as the Puritans of the Muslim world. These attitudes are in part a product of the desert culture that ruled Arabia for centuries before the coming of the Prophet Muhammad. They are also fostered by Saudi Arabia's unique role among nations as guardian of the two holiest places in all of Islam—Mecca and Medina. Islam as practiced in Saudi Arabia remains, in some ways, close to the way it was during the time of Muhammad. No alcohol is allowed, even for the nonbeliever. Pornography is strictly forbidden. Many women wear veils, and they are not allowed to drive cars. Their modesty is protected with strict rules of privacy.

Women are more active publicly in Bahrain than in most Arab countries. Great strides have been made, but life is still bounded by rules steeped in the traditions of the past. While many Bahraini women are not completely veiled, most still prefer a head covering when in public. Even long-sleeved garments are preferred over the summer sleeveless fashions of Europeans and Americans.

Bahrainis have not forsaken their Muslim traditions. Islamic laws are followed, but Bahrainis in general are very tolerant of non-Muslims who practice their own life-style in moderation. Since the new causeway was built in 1986, many Westerners who live in Saudi Arabia, and some Saudis, come to Bahrain to spend the weekend.

But while Bahrainis generally take a relaxed attitude toward the behavior of foreigners, they stress privacy and discretion for their own families.

NAMES THAT MEAN SOMETHING

It is easy to trace the genealogy of a family by its names. For example, if a father's name is Yusef, his son Abdallah will be called Abdallah bin Yusef, which means Abdallah son of Yusef. The word *bin* means "son of."

Sometimes the birth of the first son means so much to the family that the parents may become known by the child's name. For instance, if a man Hisham names his first son Saad, the man could become known as *Abu* Saad, "father of Saad;" Saad's mother would then be known as *Umm* Saad, "mother of Saad."

Knowing one's family tree is important to Arabs. Tribes are extensions of the family. Loyalty to the tribe has often been necessary for survival. Family ties are still very strong.

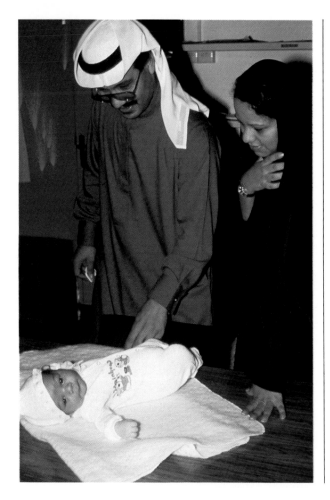

The family unit has great strength in Bahrain.

WOMEN'S ROLES

Women's lives are still centered within the family circle. A wife's role traditionally has been to support her husband and serve and care for her children. There is a remarkable strength in the family unit, and Bahraini women in numerous ways receive more respect than women in Western societies. For example, long before Western women began to keep their maiden names after marriage, this had been and remains to this day the practice of Muslim women. Moreover, in matters pertaining to property and inheritance, women in Western societies have not yet acquired some of the rights that Muslim women are provided in Islamic law. Islamic law clearly states that women need not contribute to family expenses and that they retain sole control over their money and inheritance after marriage. In Western society, women who are more able could be required to supply support for children.

Many among Bahrain's more conservative Muslim women, in deference to tradition and the values placed on modesty, prefer to wear long veils that cover their bodies from the top of their heads to their feet. When carrying a package or a child, these women have a way of folding their veil across their face and securing it with their teeth, so only their eyes show.

A comparatively significant and ever-increasing number of women have jobs outside their homes. The kinds of jobs that are considered respectable, however, are very limited. Women teach in girls' schools and work in maternity clinics and in a range of skilled positions in banks and other businesses. Very few women are employed as maids, because Bahraini families tend to import their household help from India, Pakistan, Bangladesh, Sri Lanka, and the Philippines.

MEN'S RIGHTS

Islamic law gives a Muslim man the right to have four wives, but only if he is able to treat them all equally—a standard that few can meet. The practice dates from the earliest days of Islam, when the number of women far exceeded the number of men. It was felt that such a right, practiced in exceptional circumstances, could be a humane answer to three social needs. First, it would address the needs of women who otherwise might never have a husband. Second, it would ease the process by which a widow could remarry. Third, it would help serve the needs of a child who otherwise would not have a father. Today, however, circumstances are substantially different, and fewer and fewer Bahraini men follow this tradition.

So that a child would be certain of its parentage and have its rights to inheritance protected, it was also agreed that women would not be allowed to have more than one husband.

In keeping with the goal of increasing the number of Muslims, Muslim men may marry women of other religions, whereas Muslim women are forbidden to marry non-Muslims.

DOWRIES AND DIVORCE

A groom must pay a dowry—usually a combination of money, gold, furniture, and sometimes even real estate—to the bride's family. Gold is frequently given in the form of jewelry—beautiful gold filigree necklaces, bracelets, and rings. This is usually kept in the bride's name so that if her husband should at some time decide to divorce her, she will be able to support herself and not have any need of alimony. The value of the dowry is often high. This makes Muslim marriage and, hence, also divorce, far more expensive than marriages and divorces in Western countries. The intent is to emphasize the serious commitment that marriage entails.

One of the consequences is that divorce among Muslims is far less common than in Western countries.

In Bahrain, as elsewhere, women are apt to take great care in their makeup and in grooming their hair. There are special occasions when they paint traditional designs on their hands and feet. They take the leaves from a henna bush, dry them, and make a reddish-brown paste from the residue. They paint florets and geometric patterns, usually on the palms of their hands. When the paste dries, the dye that remains will last several weeks.

Henna also is used by men who live by old-time customs. A man who has returned from a pilgrimage to Mecca is allowed to dye his beard with orange henna to announce to all that he has devoutly fulfilled one of the key obligations of being Muslim.

MARRIAGES

Parents usually arrange marriages. It is hard for a young man to pick out a wife if he has not had a chance to date her — or even see what she looks like, if she happens to wear a veil. Men and women alike have therefore long depended on the members of their families to help assess the qualities of their prospective marriage partners. One of the ways this occurs is when women gather at tea parties or weddings with other members of their sex. On such occasions young unmarried girls try to make the very best impression, for they know that the opinion of a sister, mother, or aunt of a prospective suitor can be important in determining whether a marriage offer is to be made.

Today, however, if a son or daughter does not approve of a marriage proposal, parents seldom, if ever, force such a union. Even so, it is still a matter of two people who know each other far less intimately than their counterparts in Western countries deciding to make a life together. An important compensating factor, though, is that their respective families — the cornerstones of society — are much more closely connected and supportive of one another than is typically the case with the families of the bride and the groom in Western marriages.

Young girls playing in a private courtyard wear gold bracelets and gold ornaments on their veils. Inset: Some typical gold jewelry that is available in Bahrain.

When women are by themselves, their veils are discarded, and the wealthy may be wearing the most fashionable designer clothes from Europe. In such households, because servants attend to most of the menial tasks, boredom can be a problem. In conservative families if the women want to go shopping, they usually go in groups of other women or are accompanied by a husband, brother, or other male member of the family.

Unmarried children usually live with their parents or relatives until married. This is true of all classes, whether wealthy or poor.

MEN'S DRESS

As ordered in the Koran, a Muslim man is expected to dress modestly and simply—a sign of equality among believers. He typically wears a long outer garment called a *thobe*, which extends from his neck to his ankles. Because of the warm weather, these garments are made of white cotton. On his head he wears a large rectangular piece of material called the *ghutra*, which is held in place by a thick, black, ropelike band called an *agal*. This traditional Arab dress has not changed for centuries. The headpiece was practical in the desert for protection during a sandstorm and against the sun. The headband could be used to bind two of a camel's feet to keep it from straying.

Tailoring is practically a nonexistent item in the family budget. The ruler's robe and those of high-ranking government officials are often made of a finer piece of cloth, but there is no difference in style. Wealth is manifested in other ways. In today's world, it is often demonstrated by the make of the family car and the size and style of one's home. Even so, the values of the society prize modesty and understatement, not indulgence or ostentation.

HOMES

The styles of homes vary little in design—only in size and elegance of furnishings. No wood is to be had, unless it is imported. Thick walls are built of cement and lime brick. In the cities, front doors face directly out onto streets. Rooms are built around inner courtyards.

Almost all houses are built vertically. The higher they build, the better chance to catch a breeze. In keeping with the value attached to privacy, lower rooms have very small windows that can be shuttered. Ordinarily they are left open, with ornamental metal grillwork in place. Upper stories frequently have large arched openings for ventilation.

Homes are constructed of cement and lime brick. The front doors in city houses (far left) open directly onto the street. Large arched openings in the house under construction (above) will help provide ventilation. A wind tower (left) funnels air through the lower floors of a building.

Outside the city, many houses are built in clusters surrounded by walls that afford protection against the sand, which, in certain seasons, blows for days on end.

The wind towers of Bahrain, the United Arab Emirates, and Qatar are not found on the Saudi coast. They are kiosklike dwellings, usually on the second or third floors of a building, that are constructed with shafts in such a way as to funnel wind through the lower floors. Even the poor have wind towers.

The prized furnishings of any house are the rugs, either beautiful, richly patterned Orientals from the looms of Iran across the water or the more crudely woven, but handsome, rugs made by local men, women, and children. It can take several years to knot and weave a large carpet. Smaller prayer rugs are also popular. Five times a day they are unrolled when the devout kneel and touch their heads to the ground or floor in prayer.

Rugs are passed down from one generation to the next. Wealthy businessmen frequently invest in antique rugs, which they store in vaults as a hedge against inflation. Rugs are almost a form of currency. The supply of oil may give out someday, but the skills for such masterpieces of craftsmanship are being kept alive.

DINING ARAB STYLE

The main meal of the day is the climax of Arab hospitality. If invited to share the occasion, and one is not otherwise committed or unable to accept, it is a social blunder to refuse. Meals are taken seriously and are generally conducted without conversation. The hour or more before the guests sit down to eat is the time when the host and guests converse. Accordingly, it is customary that guests leave soon after eating, but not before a cup of coffee, which signals the end of the occasion.

Coffee is the traditional welcome in any Bahraini household. These are served in small handleless cups, which are filled a third of the way so the rim can be held without burning the fingers. The coffee is unsweetened and flavored with cardamon.

A variety of fresh vegetables, lamb, and fish are available. Chicken and beef are also popular. (Muslims are forbidden to eat pork.) There is always a rice dish, but a rice different from what Westerners might be used to eating. Basmati rice is a hard-grained variety that has a slight nutty taste.

The waters of the gulf teem with shrimp, and a wide variety of fish is caught near the coral reefs just offshore. Catches have improved immeasurably since the government restricted the wholesale exploitation of the famous, fist-sized Bahraini shrimp some years ago. Bahrainis prefer to barbecue fish over glowing

Above: Coffee is served to guests in small handleless cups.
Left: Sweet pastries just out of the oven

coals though they oven bake, fry, or stew them, too.

Flat bread in the gulf is known as *khoubz*. In Manama, it is common to find khoubz baked on the walls of the *tannour*, clay ovens that look like beehives. The dough is allowed to rise in the warmth of the bakery before being rolled into sheets and baked in thirty to forty seconds to a crisp golden brown.

Samouli, a white bread similar to French bread, is baked in a conventional oven. The top is glazed with water or egg and is sprinkled with coarse salt or sesame or caraway seeds.

One of the most popular dishes of the region, which was developed by the Bedouin, is *ghouzi*. To prepare this, the cook starts with a whole lamb. Inside the lamb is placed a chicken stuffed with rice, nuts, onions, spices, and shelled hard-boiled eggs. The cavity is sewn and the lamb trussed before being roasted on a spit. When serving ghouzi, the chicken and stuffing are removed and arranged around the lamb. The diner breaks off chunks of meat with his right hand. The meat is not carved.

Chapter 9

EVERYDAY LIFE

THE LANGUAGE

Nearly 200 million people are Arabs. Millions more speak Arabic, the language of the Koran and Islamic prayers. Just under a billion people are Muslims. Islam is the fastest-growing faith in the world.

Written Arabic is a graceful combination of flowing lines that follow very definite rules. Most letters of most words are connected to the next letter.

The Islamic religion forbids the use of pictures depicting humans or animals. This was supposed to discourage people from worshiping idols, as they had in earlier times. Artists, accordingly, took the beautiful Arabic language and made many designs with the letters. They developed calligraphy to such an artistic style that words are often carved in stone or worked into mosaics as decorations on buildings. Verses are even woven into rugs.

The Arabic language bases each of its words on a three-consonant letter combination. To link these letters together, Arabs use either three short or three long vowels. All words related to one general idea will use the same three consonants. For instance, the words for "book," "library," and "write" are all spelled with k, t, and b—in that order. Only the vowels will be different.

Although it might seem that this would make learning the language easy, foreigners have found that the very inflection given a certain word, for example, spoken with the voice rising at the end of the word or dropping in tone, can change the meaning.

A LANGUAGE OF GESTURES

Like people of many other cultures, Arabs often use hand gestures to supplement the spoken language. They frequently speak not only with their mouths but also with their hands and eyes. For example, the act of putting the tips of one's fingers and thumb together, pointing them upward, and moving the hand up and down, means, "Be patient, wait a minute." To motion a person to come forward, the fingers of one's right hand are pressed together and pointed downward while moving the hand toward the person making the gesture.

While the English language and many other languages are written from left to right, Arabic language is written from right to left. What to a Westerner would be the last page of a book is to an Arab, with respect to a book that is written in Arabic, the first page.

Even Arabic numerals—the source of Western numerals—are different. A three looks a bit like a backward seven with a peak in the top line. Zero—an Arab concept introduced to mathematics— is simply a dot.

For many years speech was the only form of communication. The Prophet Muhammad, who was illiterate, had a scribe write down the revelations that he received from Allah. The sum of the revelations constitute the Koran, the holy book of Islam.

The spoken word is important and should not be taken lightly. One Islamic proverb states, "The sword wounds the body, but words wound the soul."

Some Arabs of Bedouin origin, stemming from their desert heritage in which furniture was nonexistent, are quite comfortable sitting on the floor of their homes with cushions for arm rests and pillows to support the back. Regardless of how one sits, it is impolite and a sign of disrespect for the soles of one's shoes to be pointed in the direction of another's face.

Arab men often kiss each other on both cheeks as a greeting, and walk together holding hands. This is a normal show of friendship. In a formal audience with their head of state, they will sometimes kiss him on the nose or shoulder as a sign of respect.

EDUCATION

Bahrain has long been a pioneer in education. The first school for boys to be opened in the Arabian Gulf region was the al-Hadiyya al-Khalifiya (gift of the Khalifa family) School in 1919. The first girls' school was opened in Bahrain in 1929. Their modern system of education has provided the highest literacy rate in the gulf region and, among developing countries, one of the highest in the world.

The Bahrain government has long been known for its commitment to harnessing education in general and technology in particular to development.

A music class in a boys' school (left) and a computer class in a girls' school (above)

Education is compulsory for all children. Profits from oil development were used to open teaching centers in all parts of the country. In the past, many of Bahrain's teachers were Egyptians, because the language was the same and many Egyptians were available. At the precollegiate level, there are separate centers for males and females. For the most part, courses for men and women are comparable in subject and quality of instruction. Classes are often given in conjunction with programs on television and radio.

The first major law regarding education was passed in 1975. The law increased the time required to pass the high school tests from two to three years. The Compulsory Education Law provided that education must be free and compulsory for all Bahraini and non-Bahraini children during the elementary and preparatory stages. The Private Education Law provided for the structure of private education, giving guidelines for curriculum

The University of Bahrain

content as well as for staffing levels and administrative organization.

When the Arabian Gulf nations decided to sponsor a regional Arabian Gulf University, Bahrain, centrally located along the gulf's western shore and middle-of-the road politically and socially, was selected as the logical site for the campus. An established medical school in Manama offered temporary facilities for the new university.

The university's first class, numbering 350 students, was graduated in 1989. The most modern laboratory equipment is available. Students master keyboards under banks of computer screens. The university emphasizes engineering, business management, health, computer programming, hotel and catering services, and other disciplines.

In 1991 the university was renamed the University of Bahrain,

High school students

combining what had at one time been the Gulf Polytechnical
Institute and the University College of Arts, Science, and
Education.

A special department is dedicated to desert and arid zone
sciences. Dr. Ahmed al-Agib, professor at the university, says that,
"For the first time, using the miracles of twentieth-century
technology, remote-sensing satellites, genetic engineering, solar
power, and isotope hydrology, we can hold back, even reclaim the
desert. Our graduate program is training specialists to fight this
battle."

Bahrain is developing several institutes of higher learning,
drawing on increasing pools of Bahrainis returning from abroad
with advanced degrees.

The government provides free education for all children. The
ministry of education administers 140 schools for boys and girls at
three levels.

The Salmaniya Medical Center (above) is part of Bahrain's health-care system. Medical technicians work in a laboratory (below) at the center.

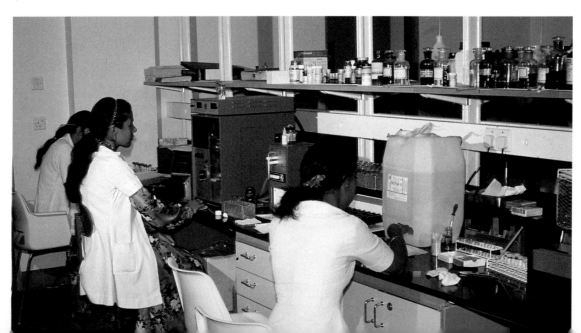

To illustrate how much the Bahraini government is counting on the next generation of educated citizens to enhance the country's future, the annual budgets for the past decade have put education at the top of the priority list.

HEALTH CARE

Bahrain University's College of Health Sciences, operating under the direction of the ministry of health, trains nurses, pharmacists, and paramedics. Bahrain offers state-of-the-art health care that is subsidized by the government. In addition to an extensive system of government clinics and hospitals, there also are many doctors in private practice and several privately run hospitals.

The foundation of the modern health services dates from 1900, when the first hospital was opened. The first government doctor was officially appointed in 1925, and the first government clinic opened eleven years later.

In 1968 the government drew up a comprehensive development plan for health services in cooperation with the World Health Organization (WHO). This included strengthening the medical services available, training medical technicians to staff the medical centers, and building up the preventive care section that coordinates health programs throughout the gulf.

The plan went into operation in 1970. The Salmaniya Medical Center has 640 beds, staffed by more than eighteen hundred highly trained employees, Bahraini and non-Bahraini. Numerous Bahrainis study abroad in preparation for duties at Salmaniya when they return.

An Arabian horse

ARABIAN HORSES

Bahrainis share the love of horse racing with their Arab neighbors. It is mainly the wealthy who own these beautifully trained Arabian horses, but there is no barrier to keep others from thrilling to the sport as breeders or spectators.

The genuine Arabian, or Kehailan, horse is the most ancient of domestic breeds. It appeared in Egyptian drawings as far back as 1500 B.C. Legend has it that the first person to mount and master the horse was Ishmael, son of Abraham. It is alleged that Ishmael was able to do this because, in this most noble of creatures, he recognized the presence of God in nature.

Great care is given to the breeding and raising of the Arabian horse. The symmetry, speed, vigor, gentleness, and endurance of this fine strain of animal have evolved by necessity in a land where conditions have traditionally been harsh. In the early days,

Riding Arabian horses in the desert

the Arab horse, like his Bedouin master, ate whatever was available—dried meat, dates, or fodder. The meager diet, interspersed with frequent periods of near starvation, refined the breed to its small stature.

The Arabian is a distinct species—*Equus arabicus*. It has good quality bones, as dense as the finest ivory, and a large skull, but fewer vertebrae and ribs than thoroughbreds.

A European traveler in Arabia in the 1820s, Johann Ludwig Burckhardt, reported that the Bedouin frequently knew the genealogy of their horses more accurately than that of their family. The mares that Burckhardt encountered were never ridden until their fourth year and were not allowed to breed before their fifth year. The Bedouins, he said, never allowed a foal to fall on the ground at the moment of its birth. The newborn was held in human arms for several hours as the owner washed and stretched the tender legs as if it were a baby.

Arabians have been prized as the fastest horses alive. "Drinkers of the wind," they were called by a celebrated ninth-century poet, al-Mutannabi. Their fame spread, but it was not until Europeans discarded their heavy battle armor in the Middle Ages that these horses were exported in large numbers to the rest of the world.

Today every horse in the English General Stud Book traces its sires to three Arabian stallions. At first the book listed every horse that performed credibly. About 1808 it was agreed that only the genealogy of royal horses should be included in the book, and the founding sires had to be those from which the three greatest racers had descended.

Matchem was foaled in 1748 and was a grandson of an Arabian horse bred in the Barbary region of Arab North Africa. The horse, originally owned by King Louis XIV of France, was a gift from the ruler of Morocco.

Herod, foaled in 1758, was a great grandson of a Turkish stallion brought to England by an Englishman named Byerly.

The greatest lineage of all was started by Eclipse, foaled in 1764. Eclipse was a great-great-grandson of an Arabian horse purchased in Syria and brought to England for training.

Today 80 percent of all thoroughbred horses can trace their breeding lines back to Eclipse. Fifteen percent are traceable to Matchem, the remainder to Herod.

Bahrain has several riding schools and sports clubs for pleasure riding. The elite spare no expense in maintaining some of the Arabian Gulf's finest stables of race horses. Horse racing is big business and one that Bahrainis can point to with pride. Not far from the capital city of Manama is a fine race track. Many a young thoroughbred is tested on this home race course. The winners frequently go on to compete in races all over the world.

Falcons are carried on the wrists of their handlers.

FALCONRY

Another island tradition is the ancient art of falconry, hunting with specially trained birds. Once it was a way of life to help hard-pressed Bedouins put food on the fire to feed their families. Now it is practiced as a sport, and an expensive one at that.

When done in the grand manner, Arabian hawking was done on horseback accompanied by lean salukis—dogs that resemble

The falcon on the right is hooded with a red leather helmet.

greyhounds. The falcons are renowned as birds of prey. They are carried on the wrists of their handlers and hooded with small leather helmets, often red or green and richly decorated with gold and silver thread.

Falconry is a fascinating sport to watch. Falcons can spiral and soar on the slightest updraft of air. Their eyes can see prey several miles away. Their talons are sharp, their feet strong enough to be able to pick up and fly off with prey that weighs almost as much as they do.

Trade restrictions and a shortage of falcons have driven up costs. A prized, well-trained bird can cost as much as $15,000. During the 1970s, an American ornithologist, supported by the heir apparent, Shaikh Hamad bin Isa, experimented in a falcon-breeding project.

In the falcon center in Zallaq, temperature and humidity-controlled chambers were built for breeding-age falcons. Peregrine

A soccer match

falcons have been successfully bred in North America, but this was the first such attempt in the Middle East. The breeding experiment met with only limited success, but the center has served other purposes, mainly as a place to which falconers bring their sick birds for treatment.

MODERN SPORTS

More modern sports include soccer, which was imported while Bahrain was a British-protected state. There are tennis courts on the islands. But because the heat and humidity do not encourage a high-spirited game, there are also indoor facilities.

The sea around the islands is ideal for water sports. Scuba diving off coral reefs is popular, but although the water can look invitingly paint-pot blue from the surface, it is often rough and muddy at the bottom.

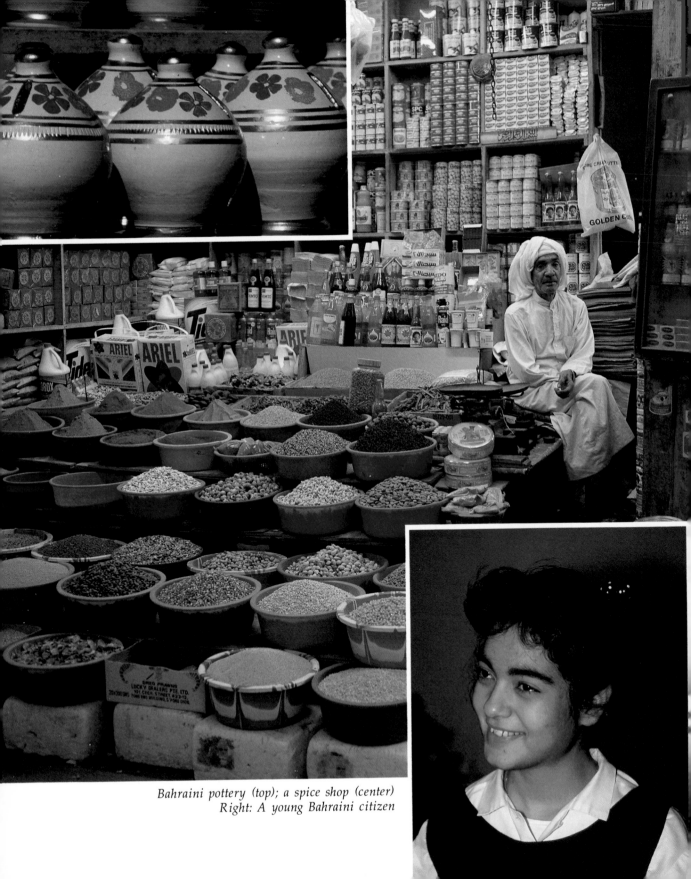

Bahraini pottery (top); a spice shop (center)
Right: A young Bahraini citizen

Apartment buildings in Manama

Every harbor has its quota of luxury boats. Some can be leased by visitors for fishing, but the more lavish yachts are used as leisure retreats.

For some, racing dune buggies now competes with camel racing. Many young Bahraini men, and some older ones too, enjoy the sport.

Many Arab families go camping together in the desert as a way to commemorate their past heritage and as a recreational retreat from the bustle of the city. On weekends it is not unusual to see tents scattered about the desert. Boys may be playing soccer in the desert instead of herding flocks of animals. It is one way that extended families of cousins, aunts, uncles, and all the generations can maintain close ties.

In such settings, a family will often build a huge bonfire and barbecue a sheep. Their ancestors would have done the same. Stories will be told and music played, the whole affair evoking a scene not so different from one played out a thousand years ago. Only the television towers and the high-rises on the horizon alter the picture.

Pride of heritage and pride in their role in applying modern technology are at the root of what, to many Bahrainis, promises to be a great future for their country.

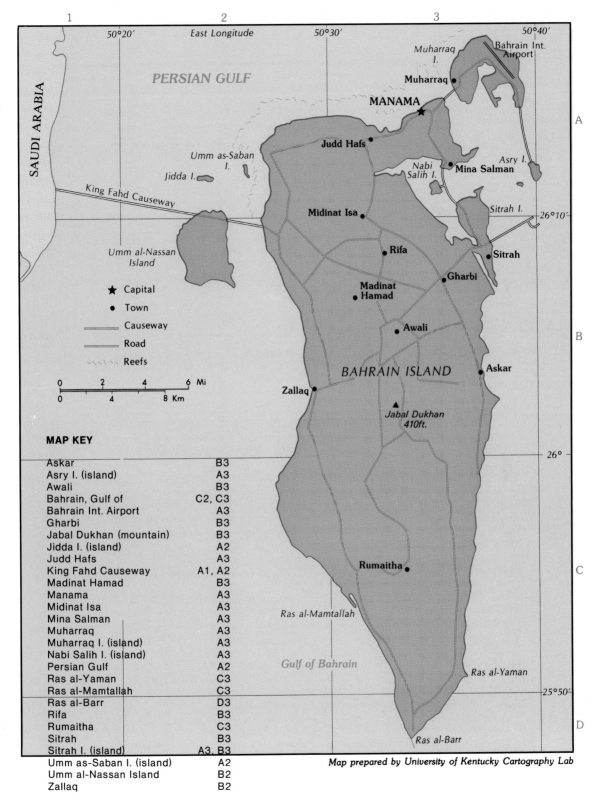

MAP KEY

Map prepared by *University of Kentucky Cartography Lab*

Opposite page: A craftsman weaves palm fronds into a basket.

MINI-FACTS AT A GLANCE

GENERAL INFORMATION

Official Name: Dawlat al-Bahrayn (State of Bahrain)

Capital: Manama

Government: Bahrain is an *emirate* ("constitutional monarchy") under the rule of the al-Khalifa family. The *emir* is the chief of state and he rules through a 15-member appointed Cabinet. The prime minister is the head of government. The emir also appoints officials called *mukhtars* ("headmen") for administration of rural communities. There are no political parties.

Since 1975 when the National Assembly was abolished, there have been no public elections; people do not have the right to vote. For administrative purposes Bahrain is divided into nine regions. There are two towns with special status—Hamad and Madinat Isa. The courts administer the legal code and review the laws to ensure their fairness. All nationalities are subject to the jurisdiction of the Bahrain courts.

Religion: Islam is the official religion. Almost 85 percent of the population follows Islam; some 70 percent are Shiite Muslims and 24 percent are Sunni Muslims; Christians (Roman Catholic and Protestant) make up about 5 percent; and the rest, less than 2 percent, are Hindus and other religions. There is a tiny indigenous Jewish community.

Ethnic Composition: Bahraini Arabs make up some 68 percent of the total population; followed by Pakistanis, Indians, and Iranians, 25 percent; Europeans, 3 percent; and other Arabs, 4 percent. Most of the noncitizen laborers are from the Indian subcontinent, South Asia, and Southeast Asia, with Indians, Pakistanis, Bangladeshis, and Filipinos being the four-largest groups.

Language: Arabic is the official language. English is the language of commerce and is spoken by a large number of people. Farsi (Persian), Hindi, and Urdu also are spoken by Iranians, Indians, and Pakistanis respectively. The Arabic language, like Farsi and Urdu, is written from right to left.

National Flag: Two versions of the national flag are officially recognized; one has a serrated white line on the staff side and the other has a straight white line. A red field covers about three-fourths of the flag.

National Emblem: The coat of arms was developed in the 1930s by a British adviser to the ruler, Sir Charles Belgrave. It is a red shield with a white serrated border at the top, surrounded by a red and white mantling.

National Anthem: "Assalam al-Amiri" ("Hail to the Emir")

National Calendar: Islamic and Gregorian

Money: The national currency is 1 Bahrain dinar of 1,000 fils. In 1992 one Bahrain dinar was equal to $2.90 in U.S. currency.

Membership in International Organizations: United Nations and most of its specialized agencies; Arab League; Gulf Cooperation Council; Organization of Arab Petroleum Exporting Countries (OAPEC)

Weights and Measures: The metric system is used but some local measures such as *tola, ruba*, and *maund* also are in use.

Population: According to the 1990 estimates, Bahrain's population was 503,000. The population is increasing at a fast rate and it is estimated to double in some 30 years; urban 82.7%; rural 17.3%. The population density was 1,882 persons per sq. mi. (726 persons per sq km).

Towns:
Manama	151,500
Muharraq	78,000
Judd Hafs	48,000
Rifa	45,000
Madinat Isa	40,000

(Population based on 1988 estimates.)

GEOGRAPHY

Borders: The Islands of Bahrain are surrounded by the waters of the Persian (Arabian) Gulf.

Coastline: 78 mi. (126 km)

Land: Bahrain is an archipelago consisting of some 33 islands in the Persian (Arabian) Gulf between the Qatar Peninsula and Saudi Arabia. Only five of these 33 islands are inhabited. The total land area is 262 sq. mi. (678 sq km) including the Hawar Islands—about four times the size of Washington, D.C. Almost 85 percent of the land is under sand plains and salt marshes. The main island of Bahrain has a low interior plateau with one hill, Jabal Dukhan, in the central part. Most of the lesser islands are flat, dry, and sandy.

Highest Point: Jabal Dukhan at 445 ft. (136 m)

Lowest Point: Sea level

Climate: The climate is hot and humid from April to October and temperate from November to March. During summer, daytime temperatures regularly reach 106° F. (41° C); winter temperatures range from 50° F. (10° C) to about 80° F (27° C). Rainfall averages less than 4 in. (10.2 cm) and is concentrated in the winter months. Southwestern winds, *gaws*, cause periodic dust storms.

Rivers: There are no permanent rivers.

Forests and Wildlife: There are no forests in Bahrain. Some date-palm groves and occasional patches of desert shrubs and grasses are found on the northern coasts and on Nabih Salih island. Wild desert flowers appear for a short time after rains. Desert rats, some gazelles, mongooses, lizards, snakes, and rabbits make up the mammalian life. Bird life includes larks, swallows, bulbuls, parakeets, and thrushes. At al-Andareen, Bahrain has built a world-class refuge for a wide variety of wildlife such as different kinds of exotic birds, plus gazelles, oryx, and ibex. Most of the animals are native to the region and nearby areas, and some animals are considered to be endangered species.

Greatest Distances: North to south: 50 mi. (80 km)
East to west: 26 mi. (42 km)

ECONOMY AND INDUSTRY

Agriculture: Only 3.5 percent of the total land area is under cultivation and permanent crops, and an additional 7 percent is under some kind of meadows and pastures. Scarcity of water and salinity of the soil limits agricultural activity. Fruits, watermelons, dates, tomatoes, eggplants, onions, and cucumbers are grown on the northern coast. Spring water from several freshwater springs in the northern part of the island is used for irrigation. Domesticated animals include goats, sheep, and cattle. Chickens provide almost all of the eggs and about half of the poultry needs of the country. Bahrain is surrounded by one of the largest pearl oyster beds, but pearl diving is almost extinct now. More than 300 species of fish are found in Bahraini waters off the coast. Fish and shrimp are caught in the coastal waters mostly for local use.

Mining: The chief energy products are petroleum and natural gas. Bahrain was the first Arab gulf country to discover oil, and was the first with an oil refinery. According to a treaty, Abu Safah offshore oil fields are operated solely by Saudi Arabia, but Bahrain collects half of Abu Safah's oil revenues. It is estimated that at the present rate of consumption, Bahrain's natural gas supply will last until about the year 2050. Gas is the primary energy used to run Bahrain's power stations, desalination plants, and aluminum smelting plants. Bahrain does not produce any coal.

Manufacturing: Fuel oil, aviation gasoline, naphtha, kerosene, heavy lubricant distillate, petroleum bitumen, liquefied petroleum gas, aluminum metal, methanol, plastics, and paper are the chief products. Bahrain also has started manufacturing instruments for petrochemical and oil-refining plants. There are several water desalination and electrical plants. The Arab Shipbuilding and Repair Yard complex is one of the largest in the Middle East. The Sitrah Oil Refinery, once one of the largest and most modern in the world, is scheduled to be refurbished and expanded in the mid-1990s. A large industrial zone is established close to the port of Mina Salman. Handicrafts, woodwork, and other light industries are encouraged by the government. Wooden *dhows* (small boats) are still produced in the same style that has been in use since nearly 3000 B.C.

Transportation: There are no railroads or internal waterways. The total length of roads in the early 1990s was 182 mi. (293 km). Gulf Air is the international airline which is jointly administered by the governments of Bahrain, Oman, Qatar, and the Emirate of Abu Dhabi. The international airport at Muharraq is served by some 22 airlines.

Numerous shipping services link Bahrain with Europe, the U.S., India, Pakistan, China, Japan, and Australia. The main dry dock at port Mina Salman is one of the largest in the world. Bahrain Island is connected by a causeway with Muharraq island in the north, and by a bridge with Sitrah island in the east. A four-lane highway over 15 mi. (24 km) long, King Fahd Causeway, connects Bahrain with Saudi Arabia to the west. The new town of Madinat Hamad is connected with roads to other cities.

Communication: Bahrain has one of the most modern communication systems in the world. The telecommunications facilities include direct-dial telephone service to some 50 countries, telegraph, telex, fax, and data-base exchange. Six daily newspapers and several magazines are published both in Arabic and English. Bahraini television features Arabic and English-language programs.

Banking and Trade: Bahrain is a strong regional banking and commercial center. In the early 1990s some 60 international offshore (tax exempt) banks were operating in Bahrain; these banks are not involved in local banking, but help channel money from the petroleum producing countries into the world market. Bahrain is also the Middle East headquarters of many large international companies.

Imports and Exports: The chief import items are machinery, industrial equipment, motor vehicles, clothing, and foodstuffs. The major import sources are Saudi Arabia, Japan, the United States, Great Britain, Italy, Australia, and Germany. The chief exports are petroleum, aluminum products, and fish; major export destinations are Japan, India, Singapore, the United States, United Arab Emirates, and Canada.

EVERYDAY LIFE

Health: An extensive system of government clinics and hospitals provide free modern health care to all. Smallpox has been totally eradicated. Mass inoculations in rural areas, better sewer and piped water facilities, and access to health clinics have greatly improved the national health. There are many private doctors and hospitals. Patients needing special care are sent abroad at the government's expense.

Education: Bahrain has one of the highest literacy rates in the Middle East. In the early 1990s the literacy rate was more than 90 percent.

Education is free and compulsory at the primary level. Primary education lasts from six to 11 years of age; secondary from 12 to 17 years of age. Attendance in primary schools is close to 100 percent. Schools are separate for boys and girls. There are 9 vocational and teacher-training institutes, and several religious schools. The University of Bahrain is at Manama. The College of Health Sciences trains nurses, pharmacists, and paramedics. The university colleges of Arts and Sciences, Education, Engineering, and Management and Business Administration were combined in 1986.

Holidays:

> New Year's Day, January 1
> National Day, December 16

Muslim holidays are based on the Islamic lunar calendar and may vary from year to year. Movable Muslim holidays are Muharram (Muslim New Year), 'Ashoura (the Prophet's Birthday), 'Id al-Fitr, and 'Id al-'Adha.

Culture: Manama is a good mixture of past and present. Modern glass buildings stand side by side with historic mosques and tall minarets. Whereas half a century ago donkeys and occasionally camels were still used for transportation in the rural areas, a wide range of modern cars are a common site not only within the city business center but throughout the country as well. There are some 10 public libraries. The National Museum at Manama, which opened in 1986, houses a world class facility that is second to none in the entire gulf area.

Life-style: A Bahraini Muslim's life-style is determined by the rules of the Koran, the Muslim's holy book. The family is the cornerstone of Bahraini society and family ties are very strong. Traditional Arab dress is still popular, but Western influence in clothing is increasing.

Muslim women, as a symbol of modesty, generally wear a scarf or other form of head covering. In keeping with age-old customs and traditions, most marriages are arranged by the bride and groom's parents with the couple's consent. Muslim men may marry women of other religions, but Muslim women are forbidden to marry non-Muslims. Also, Islamic law, which was formulated in the earliest days of the Prophet Muhammad, when women far outnumbered men, allows a Muslim man to have four wives provided that he is able to treat each one, in affection as well as attention and material goods, with absolute equality. Since the qualifying conditions are very difficult for most people to meet, the actual number of Muslim men who have more than one wife is minuscule. In order to leave no question regarding the paternity of children, which is critical to an individual's right to inheritance, women by contrast are allowed to have only one husband at a time.

Housing: Bahrainis enjoy one of the highest standards of living in the gulf region. Most of the population lives in cities and towns in the northern part of Bahrain Island. The thatch huts of earlier times have long since been replaced by cement houses and modern apartment complexes. Since there is no local production of wood, all wood used in houses is imported. A traditional architectural feature is the construction of rooms around courtyards. Rooms on the lower floors typically have small windows while upper stories often have large arched openings for ventilation. In the modern houses air conditioning and refrigerators are common.

A new town, Madinat Hamad has been built on a plateau in the center of the island, housing close to 100 thousand Bahrainis. Twelve thousand homes were built under contract to the ministry of housing. The town has a large hospital, clinics, schools, community centers, a library, police and fire stations, several mosques, and numerous playgrounds.

Food: A typical Bahraini meal will have a rice dish, accompanied with a flat bread, vegetables, lamb, fish, chicken, or beef. Pious Muslims do not eat pork or drink alcohol. A traditional dish is *ghouzi*—a whole roasted lamb stuffed with chicken, rice, and eggs. Coffee is taken unsweetened with cardamon and is served in small handleless cups.

Sports and Recreation: There is a fine race track near Manama, and several riding schools and sports clubs for horse riding. Falconry is the ancient art of hunting with specially trained birds. It is an expensive sport and a well-trained bird can cost as much as $15,000. Sick birds are treated at the Falcon Center at Zallaq. Modern sports include soccer, tennis, and racing dune buggies. Water sports, such as scuba diving off coral reefs, are popular. Camping in the desert is a recreation enjoyed by many Bahraini families.

Social Welfare: Social welfare programs were established by the government as far back as the 1920s and 1930s. Better schools and hospitals were built and better working conditions were provided for laborers. Food and essential commodities are subsidized for poor families; they also receive subsistence allowances from the Ministry of Labor and Social Affairs. All public employees are covered by a social security system. A Social Security Law covers pensions, industrial accidents, sickness, unemployment, maternity, and family allowance.

IMPORTANT DATES

3000 B.C. —Irrigation *qanats* (underground tunnels that carry water by gravity flow) are built in Bahrain

A.D. 1521—Portuguese declare the territory of Bahrain a possession of Portugal

1602—Portuguese are forced out by Bahrainis with the help of other Arabs

1782—The al-Khalifa Arab family drive the Persians away from Bahrain

1820—A general treaty is signed by the British and some Persian (Arabian) Gulf states including Bahrain (later revised in 1861, 1892, and 1951); it is decided that the friendly Arab states should all have a red flag with a white border

1861—Bahrain becomes a British Protected State (ends in 1971)

1900—The first hospital is opened

1908—Oil is discovered in Iran

1919—The first school for boys in the Arab gulf region is opened in Bahrain

1922 — Major Frank Holmes negotiates a deal with Saudi Arabia for exploratory oil drilling

1925 — The first government doctor is appointed

1928 — Iran renews claim on Bahrain

1929 — One pearl found in the gulf water is sold for about $100,000; soon after, the introduction of cultured pearls by the Japanese signals the rapid demise of Bahrain's natural pearl industry, deepening the local dimensions of the international economic Depression; the first school for girls is opened

1931 — Bahrain's first oil well is drilled at Jabal Dukhan

1935 — The first oil refinery is constructed on the Arab side of the gulf

1938 — Territorial dispute over Hawar Islands between Qatar and Bahrain is decided in Bahrain's favor

1942 — Shaikh Salman bin Hamad al-Khalifa becomes ruler of Bahrain

1948 — The state of Israel is created

1949 — Bahrain becomes headquarters for U.S. Middle East forces, a modest symbolic manifestation of official U.S. support for the security of the Gulf Arab States

1956 — Widespread rioting breaks out demanding more local participation in Bahraini government

1958 — Bahrain becomes a free port

1960 — The industrial zone near port Mina Salman is opened; free health services for both citizens and noncitizens starts

1961 — The present emir, Shaikh Isa bin Salman al-Khalifa, becomes head of state

1962—The new port of Mina Salman is opened

1965—Major industrial strike erupts following introduction by the Bahrain Petroleum Company (Bapco) of labor-saving devices that render the company more cost effective, efficient, and profitable but, also, entails termination of employment for many Bahrainis

1967—Upon British withdrawal from the Crown Colony of Aden, Bahrain becomes headquarters for the British Middle East Force Command

1968—Great Britain announces its intention to terminate its treaties of protection with several Gulf Arab states by 1971; Bahrain's first satellite station is installed; a comprehensive plan for health services is charted; Bahrain, Qatar, and the Trucial States form the Federation of Arab Emirates

1970—Bowing to the wishes of the Bahraini people as expressed to a representative of the United Nations Secretary General, Iran abandons its long-standing claim to Bahrain; oil production reaches its peak at 76 thousand barrels a day; the National Health Plan goes into operation with the opening of Salmaniya Medical Center

1971—Bahrain becomes an independent state on August 15; British troops withdraw from naval facilities at Jufair, in Manama; Bahrain joins the United Nations and the Arab League; a new terminal is added to the international airport

1972—The national flag is officially adopted; the country's first constitution is approved

1973—The constitution is adopted; first elections take place; television broadcasting begins; Bahrain Monetary Agency is established

1975—The National Assembly is disbanded by an emiri decree (new elections have not taken place since); the government announces the introduction of offshore (tax exempt) banking

1976—*Akhbar Al-Khalij,* the first daily Arabic newspaper, begins publishing;

International Parliamentary Union expels Bahrain for autocratic dissolution of Parliament

1978 — *The Gulf Daily News,* the country's first English daily newspaper, begins publishing

1980 — Sixty percent of the oil refinery is sold to the Bahrain Petroleum Company (Bapco); Bahrain's second satellite station is installed; a wildlife sanctuary is established

1981 — Gulf Cooperation Council (GCC) is established (members include Bahrain, Kuwait, Saudi Arabia, Qatar, Oman, and the United Arab Emirates); an Iranian-backed coup is thwarted in the emirate

1982 — The Arabian Gulf University opens; Bahrain accedes to the chairmanship and presidency of the GCC's Supreme Council and Monetarial Council for one year; Bahrain signs a security pact with Saudi Arabia

1986 — Bahrain is linked with Saudi Arabia by a causeway; Bahrain reaches an agreement with Saudi Arabia about the Abu Safah oil fields

1987 — Abu Safah oil field is closed down; Bahrain again becomes head of the GCC's highest decision-making and policy-forming bodies for one year

1988 — Three Bahrainis are convicted by the security court for their involvement in an Iranian-backed plot to overthrow the Bahraini government; a cease-fire is reached by Iraq and Iran after eight years of the Gulf War

1989 — The first class of the Arabian Gulf University graduates; a stock exchange is opened; diplomatic relations are established with the People's Republic of China; Bahrain, together with Oman and Kuwait, participates in a GCC commission in accessing political developments in the Soviet Union and the Eastern Bloc, and the ending of the Cold War, in terms of their potential impact on developments in the gulf region.

1990 — Iraq invades Kuwait; Bahrain grants the United States and Great Britain expanded access to its naval and air force facilities; Bahrain hosts thousands of displaced Kuwaitis and opens its schools to Kuwaiti students and teachers; diplomatic relations are established with the U.S.S.R. and Czechoslovakia; Shaikh Muhammad bin Mubarak al-Khalifa, the foreign minister since 1971, becomes the dean of all the world's foreign ministers

1991—Units of the Bahrain Defense Force participate in the liberation of Kuwait; Bahrain assists in the rebuilding of Kuwait's infrastructure and economy; Bahrain signs agreement with the U.S. to permit expanded logistical and operational support in the event of any future threat to Bahrain or any other GCC member country's sovereignty, independence, or territorial integrity; Bahrain-American Friendship Society is established; U.S.-Bahrain Business Council is established; Shaikh Isa visits Washington, D.C. and meets with President Bush; lacking the necessary level of ongoing financial support from other Arab gulf countries (with the exception of Saudi Arabia), the University of Bahrain assumes control of the facilities of the Arabian Gulf University

1992—Bahrain and Qatar, with the assistance of Saudi Arabia as mediator, continue to pursue a satisfactory solution to their conflicting claims to the Hawar Islands

IMPORTANT PEOPLE

Shaikh Hamad bin Isa al-Khalifa, Shaikh Isa's eldest son, crown prince, and commander in chief of Bahrain defense force; the new town of Madinat Hamad is named after him

Shaikh Isa bin Ali al-Khalifa (d.1923), ruler of Bahrain from 1868 to 1932

Shaikh Isa bin Salman al-Khalifa (1933-   ), emir of Bahrain since 1961

Shaikh bin Salman al-Khalifa, prime minister of Bahrain, brother of the present emir

Shaikh Muhammad bin Mubarak al-Khalifa, foreign minister of Bahrain

Shaikh Salman bin Hamad al-Khalifa (d.1961), ruled Bahrain from 1942 to 1961

Alfonso d'Albuquerque (1453-1515), Portuguese admiral who established colonies in Bahrain and along the coasts of Africa and India as well as in

Muscat, Oman, and Hormuz, an island in the Hormuz Straits that constitute the gateway to and from the gulf

Alexander the Great (356-323 B.C.), Greek conqueror; defeated Persians at the Battle of Issus in 333 B.C.

Johann Ludwig Burckhardt (1784-1817), a European traveler and explorer of Arabia; wrote about Arabian horses

Christoper Columbus (1451-1506), Italian navigator; discovered America in 1492

Vasco da Gama (c.1460-1524), sailor and navigator; with substantial assistance from the famous Arab navigator Ahmad bin Majid, of Oman, found and sailed across the Indian Ocean (from the Cape of Good Hope, in South Africa to India)

Major Frank Holmes, a New Zealand entrepreneur whose work led to the discovery of oil in Bahrain

Muhammad (570-632), prophet of Islam

INDEX

Page numbers that appear in boldface type indicate illustrations

About the Author

Mary Virginia Fox was graduated from Northwestern University in Evanston, Illinois, and now lives near Madison, Wisconsin, across the lake from the state capitol and the University of Wisconsin. She is the author of more than two dozen books for young adults and has had a number of articles published in adult publications.

Mrs. Fox and her husband have lived overseas for several months at a time and enjoy traveling. She considers herself a professional writer and an amateur artist. She has also written *Tunisia*, *New Zealand*, and *Iran* in the Enchantment of the World series.